What Others Are S

Worship In Song is one of the most insightful *expansions* *worship that I have ever read. Pastor Scott Aniol harmonizes the concepts of God's beauty, aesthetics, affection for God, accurate theology, and musical expertise unlike any other book on this subject. I enthusiastically recommend Worship In Song as a must read for pastors, church music directors, and all Christian musicians who sincerely desire to lead their congregations to worship God in spirit and in truth.*

Michael W. Harding
Senior Pastor, First Baptist Church
Troy, Michigan

Worship in Song may not always be an easy read, but it should become a must read for those seeking answers to tough questions about music. The book is well written, well researched, and well documented. Arguments are clearly presented. Scott Aniol takes the reader to Scripture for answers; the use of secular sources is appropriate and necessary. He is gracious and uncompromising, balanced and fair.

Ed Dunbar
Chairman, Division of Music, Bob Jones University
Greenville, South Carolina

Unhappily, the controversy about worship style has degenerated into arguments based on personal preference, particularly regarding what kind of music is acceptable. Far too frequently, advocates for both "contemporary music" and "traditional music," while giving verbal testimony to their concern for God's glory, defend their positions with man-centered reasoning. Although proponents of neither position would admit it, what pleases people often takes precedence over any consideration of what pleases the Lord. Scott Aniol's treatment of this hot topic is refreshingly and delightfully different. Throughout, his analysis is God-focused, biblically based, thought provoking, and practical. He argues convincingly that music is not neutral and that there are indeed music styles that have infiltrated the church that are absolutely inappropriate for acceptable service unto the Lord. I highly recommend Worship in Song for any who are serious about worshiping the Lord in keeping with the beauty of His holiness, especially in song—an integral element in biblical worship.

Michael P. V. Barrett
President, Geneva Reformed Seminary
Greenville, South Carolina

Scott Aniol provides a tremendous service to all who would seek to please the Lord Jesus Christ in their thoughts and emotions and in that place where their thoughts and emotions are drawn together to please God—their worship. This book is scripturally, logically, and carefully crafted. The tone of each page is gracious. The documentation of the work is clear. Best of all, the content of this book is readable and memorable. Here is a volume well suited for those who would instruct others formally but also of great value to all who would honestly ask, "How can I know how my musical selections honor God?"

Chuck Phelps
President, Maranatha Baptist College
Watertown, Wisconsin

Scott Aniol is at once theologian, historian, philosopher, aesthetician, musician, logician, and pastor in this encapsulating must-read entry in the worship wars. His biblical and musical insights are remarkable for any one person to make. As a trained musician, he brings a musical precision to the discussion that adds a practical working perspective to his theological expertise.

Tim Shafer
Professor of Piano, Penn State University

Here we have a brief and thoughtful theology of the use and place of music in the gathered worship of the people of God. Aniol argues that our current confusions over music in public worship are at the root, theological. Consequently, we need to understand what worship is (biblically), how sanctification happens, the nature and importance of religious affections, the relationship between God's glory and beauty, and the purpose of music in corporate worship before we are in a position to evaluate the kinds of music most appropriate to that purpose. When it comes to musical forms, most evangelicals *just don't think that they matter in the end, and hence drop back to their own preferences as the benchmarks of what we do and don't do musically in public services of worship. Aniol wants to challenge that approach. Rightly so.*

J. Ligon Duncan III
Senior Minister, First Presbyterian Church,
Reformed Theological Seminary, Jackson, Mississippi

In the 20 years I have been in Christian broadcasting, no single issue has been more explosive than the subject of Christian music in the church. Scott Aniol's much-needed book takes on this issue in an incisive manner, and he rightly points to the foundational issue of religious affections that underlies the entire debate. Christians have allowed Hollywood and popular culture to shape their affections, rather than Holy Scripture. As a result, they have made God over into someone who will accommodate their profane and carnal musical tastes in worship. Aniol's thoroughly biblical approach is centered on the belief that God does have something to say about the music we listen to and the music we use in worship. Christians owe a debt of gratitude to the author for his scholarship and clarity on this essential subject.

Ingrid Schlueter
Host, Crosstalk Radio Talk Show
VCY America Radio Network

Scott exemplifies personally the God-centered music philosophy he's urging upon churches corporately. He's become known for his gracious, scriptural conservatism, movingly ministered through beautiful music wed to sound theology. I rejoice that the Lord has burdened him to help churches develop even more scriptural conviction and passion for Christ through its music ministries.

Mark Minnick
Senior Pastor, Mt. Calvary Baptist Church,
Greenville, South Carolina

Scott Aniol has joined a growing chorus. In so doing he has significantly raised the rhetoric to a new level of systematic and meticulous evaluation while allying himself with those concerned believers who question the mood, sensibility, and impact of current popular worship music.

WORSHIP IN SONG
A Biblical Approach to Music and Worship

Scott Aniol

BMH BOOKS
Winona Lake, Indiana
www.bmhbooks.com

Worship in Song, a Biblical Approach to Music and Worship

Copyright © 2009 by Scott Aniol

Published by BMH Books
P.O. Box 544, Winona Lake, IN 46590 USA
www.bmhbooks.com

ISBN 978-0-88469-262-1
RELIGION / Christian Rituals Practice / Worship & Liturgy

Printed in the United States of America

To

Michael Harding and Stephen Allen
Whose theological and musical influences upon me are profound

and

My dear wife, Becky
Who patiently and lovingly gave ear to all my thoughts
before they were fully formulated

Worship Wars and Warriors

Kevin T. Bauder

Worship wars. It's a new phrase, but it expresses a phenomenon that has been around as long as people have deviated from the true worship of the living God. Sometimes the worship wars have involved actual, physical warfare, including the shedding of blood. Other times they have involved the assertion of ideas and the exercise of liturgical authority.

Worship wars have been fought over at least two kinds of issues. The first issue is, "Whom shall we worship?" The biblical answer to this question is contained in the Shema and the Great Commandment: "Hear, O Israel: The LORD our God is one LORD: And thou shalt love the LORD thy God with all thine heart, and with all thy soul, and with all thy might" (Deut. 6:4-5). In other words, one and only one being exists to whom worship is rightly directed. That one is Yahweh, the LORD, the God of the Bible.

Any effort to direct worship toward any other god than the God of the Bible is idolatrous, and it invokes the displeasure of the LORD—for "I the LORD thy God am a jealous God" (Ex. 20:5). Even when an idol is called by the name of the LORD, it remains an idol. We must worship God as the Bible reveals Him to be, resisting every attempt to remake Him in our own image or according to our own wishes.

Anyone who erects an idol in the name of the true and living God is likely to provoke a worship war. Moses went to war with the golden calf that Aaron proclaimed to be Israel's "Elohim." Paul pronounced his anathema upon anyone who declared a gospel that contradicted the true work and nature of the living God. Perhaps the greatest worship warrior of all time was Jesus Himself. He made it clear that people had to choose to perform their religious exercises either for the true and living God or else for the praise of men—but they could not do both! He insisted that people who pursued religion for human recognition were hypocrites who already had their reward. He pronounced woe upon such hypocrites, especially upon the scribes and Pharisees who ought to have known better. With Jesus, worship war became physical confrontation when He drove the hypocrites out of the temple. "The zeal of thine house hath eaten me up" (John 2:17).

Worship wars are fought over the worship of false gods. But worship wars are also fought over a second issue. Besides asking *whom* we ought to worship, we must also ask *how* we ought to worship.

Worship does not exist for the sake of the worshiper, but for the glory of the God Who is worshiped. That being the case, the most significant question in every worship event must be, "What will please God?" When we truly worship, we do not seek to please ourselves, but to please the God to Whom our worship is directed.

How do we know what pleases God? How do we know what He wishes us to offer Him in worship? To put it very simply, He tells us. Unless He tells us, we have no way to know. Therefore, we must search the Scriptures to discover what elements God authorizes us to include in our worship. Whatever elements He requires of us, we are obligated to offer. If we offer elements that He does not require, then we must not pretend that we are offering them to please Him, for how can we know that these elements please Him if He has not told us? We might rightly ask ourselves the question of Isaiah, "Who hath required this at thy hand?" (Isa. 1:12).

Nevertheless, some people do offer elements in their worship that God has not required. Why would they do such a thing? By definition, they cannot be doing it to please God. Therefore, they must be doing it to please either themselves or other people. For such worshipers, the act of worship becomes a façade to conceal either the gratification of their own appetites or the appeal for human favor. Whether they are self-pleasers or men-pleasers, their worship is the most crass idolatry. This manner of worship is an exercise in self-assertion that the apostle Paul names as "will worship" (Col. 3:23).

Even the elements that God does command can be offered in better and worse ways. If we are serious about pleasing God, we shall choose the better ways. We shall eliminate any expression of worship that debases or trivializes holy things.

Why should we be concerned about debased or trivial expressions? First, because a trivial God is not the God of the Bible. If we are trivializing God and the things of God in our worship, we are effectively transforming Him into a different God. Since the trivial god who results from this transformation is not the God of the Bible, He must be a God of our own invention: a diminutive and sometimes laughable deity. This, too, is idolatry.

Second, we are explicitly forbidden in Scripture to take the name of the LORD our God in vain. To take the LORD's name in vain means to speak of God in an empty, thoughtless, or shallow fashion. In other words, trivial or debasing expressions of worship have the effect of profaning holy things and violating the third commandment. Violating this commandment is especially serious—the LORD Himself tells us that He will not hold those guiltless who take His name in vain.

Of course, any expression may take the name of the LORD in vain. Not merely our worship, but our instruction, our fellowship, and even our witness may be profane. Reverencing the name of the LORD (treating His name as it ought to be treated) should be a major concern in all of our speech. Never should we utter corrupt communication, especially about holy things.

One of the major vehicles through which we express worship (not to mention fellowship, instruction, and witness) is music. Not surprisingly, music has come to be *the* focus of the worship wars. The reason is that the message of music is not so much propositional content as affection. That is what makes music such a powerful medium of communication. It is also why people become so attached to "their" music—the music is an externalization of what is in their souls. To criticize the music they love is to criticize their very capacity for loving. Furthermore, this affective aspect of musical communication is precisely what gives music such a powerful capacity to debase or trivialize the objects that it examines.

If our music of worship leads us to view God in the wrong way, or if it leads us to feel wrongly about God (to direct toward Him the wrong kind of love, fear, or joy, for example), then we will profane the Holy One by taking His name in vain. If we take His name in vain, then He will not hold us guiltless.

God's people must make sound judgments about the music they use to express their faith. Nothing has become more common, however, than the jibe that these judgments are "merely" matters of taste or opinion. No one disputes that they really are matters of taste and opinion. It does not follow, though, that they are purely relative. Opinion can be either right (in which case it is called *orthodoxy*) or wrong (in which case it is called *heterodoxy*). Taste, especially when directed toward holy things, can be either good (ordinate and orthopathic) or else bad (inordinate and heteropathic).

How are Christians supposed to discern when their music is orthodox and orthopathic? This is the point at which Scott Aniol enters the conversation. He understands the problems connected with the worship wars. Particularly, he understands the difficulty that confronts Christian people whose sensibilities have already been degraded by the profane. He articulates a coherent theory that, if consistently employed, would bring believers close to a mode of worship that reflects ordinate affection and orthopathic worship. In the process he responds to most of the clichés that populist evangelicals use to reinforce their prejudices.

Aniol is paddling against the current of contemporary, evangelical sensibility. Many will be so offended by his conclusions that they will never even consider his arguments. Others will examine the arguments only in the hopes of locating some weakness that they might use to refute it. That is a pity, because the issues that he raises are important and the answers that he provides are reasonable.

Scott Aniol is a worship warrior in the very best tradition. He is kind, reasonable, and careful, while also expressing strong convictions in view of the evidence. He deserves to receive a hearing.

Kevin T. Bauder, President
Central Baptist Theological Seminary
Minneapolis, Minnesota

Preface

Wars are raging. These are not the wars of flesh and blood, but of ideas—ideas about music and its role in the church.

Many books have been written on both sides of the issue. The Contemporary Christian Music debate is a hot topic on Christian bookshelves. Men like John Blanchard and Peter Anderson,[1] Frank Garlock and Kurt Woetzel,[2] Calvin Johansson,[3] Tim Fisher,[4] and John Makujina[5] have voiced arguments against the movement. Conversely, men such as Steve Miller[6] and Harold Best[7] have vigorously defended CCM. In 1997 John Frame composed a defense of what he calls "Contemporary Worship Music," a subset of CCM.[8] The battle over worship rages on, and music is the battleground.

---

[1] *Pop Goes the Gospel: Rock in the Church* (Darlington, England: Evangelical Press, 1989).

[2] *Music in the Balance* (Greenville, S.C.: Majesty Music, 1992).

[3] *Discipling Music Ministry: Twenty-First Century Directions* (Peabody, Mass.: Hendrickson, 1992).

[4] *The Battle for Christian Music* (Greenville, S.C.: Sacred Music Services, 1992).

[5] *Measuring the Music* (Salem, Ohio: Schmul, 2000).

[6] *The Contemporary Christian Music Debate: Worldly Compromise or Agent of Renewal?* (Wheaton: Tyndale House, 1993).

[7] *Music Through the Eyes of Faith* (San Francisco: Harper, 1993).

[8] *Contemporary Worship Music: A Biblical Defense* (Phillipsburg, N.J.: P & R, 1997).

So why another book on the topics of music and worship? First, few books have been written that carefully distinguish between secular music that we listen to everyday—at home, on the radio, or on our iPods—and sacred music. Certainly no firm sacred/secular distinction exists for the believer, but many books on music apply to everyday music choices principles from Scripture such as descriptions of temple worship. I am convinced that when it comes to the secular music we enjoy, much greater latitude exists than with music used for sacred purposes. For this reason, I have divided this book into two sections. After discussing some foundational matters, the first section considers how to make God-pleasing choices regarding the secular music we listen to, and the second deals more narrowly with sacred music.

The second reason I chose to write another book on music and worship is that, for a variety of reasons, newer generations are increasingly rejecting conventional arguments for a conservative music philosophy. I believe it is time for another voice. I am building upon a foundation laid by godly men whom I greatly respect, but I want to provide for the next generation a fresh, biblical approach to these serious issues.

I contend that confusion about the music issue is primarily theological, rising out of a misunderstanding of several important biblical doctrines:

- What does *Sola Scriptura* really mean?
- The nature of biblical sanctification
- The importance of biblical affections
- The biblical relationship between the glory of God and beauty
- The essence of biblical worship
- The purpose of music in the church

These doctrinal misunderstandings are compounded when we misunderstand certain cultural issues:

- Meaning in music
- The nature of pop culture
- Different kinds of emotion

We will consider each of these important matters in logical sequence. Some chapters are more practical, while others are somewhat technical. Each, in my opinion, is important in helping us make right decisions in the areas of music and worship. It is my prayer that dealing with these issues biblically and logically will give us a fresh understanding of God's desires for worship and music in these confusing times.

On a practical note, each chapter concludes with aids for further discussion so this book may be used in small groups and classrooms. Additionally, visit www.worshipinsongbook.com for resources for further study on these topics. Content there is regularly updated.

Scott Aniol
November 2008
Greenville, South Carolina
www.worshipinsongbook.com

Table of Contents

SECTION I
Laying the Foundation

CHAPTER ONE

Biblical Authority in Matters of Faith and Practice

The great sixteenth century Reformer, Martin Luther, fought against the Roman Catholic Church to recover biblical orthodoxy. His efforts resulted in the recovery of the five *Solas*: *Solus Christus* (Christ alone), *Sola Fide* (faith alone), *Sola Gratia* (grace alone), *Soli Deo Gloria* (the glory of God alone), and perhaps the most foundational, *Sola Scriptura* (Scripture alone).

In contrast to Roman Catholics who find equal authority in both Scripture and tradition, Protestants believe the Bible is the supreme authority in matters of faith and practice. Wayne Grudem summarizes the doctrine of *Sola Scriptura* well: "The sufficiency of Scripture means that Scripture contained all the words of God he intended for his people to have at each stage of redemptive history, and that it now contains all the words of God we need for salvation, for trusting him perfectly, and for obeying him perfectly." [1]

In summary, the Bible is sufficient as the ultimate authority for a Christian in all matters of faith and practice. All three primary terms in this summary are important—*authority*, *faith*, and

---

[1] Wayne Grudem, *Systematic Theology* (Grand Rapids: Zondervan, 1994), 127.

practice. (Only the written Word of God is the final authority for the Christian) This authority applies to doctrinal issues—whether belief in the virgin birth, justification by faith alone, or the hypostatic union of Christ—and it applies to practice, also.

Belief in *Sola Scriptura* flows directly from the doctrine of inspiration. The 66 books of the Old and New Testament are inspired—literally, "God-breathed." Only the original manuscripts were inspired, but subsequent manuscripts and translations are inspired in a derivative sense to the degree that they accurately reflect the words and truth of the original autographs. Human authors were "carried along" miraculously through the work of the Holy Spirit (2 Peter 1:21) such that the authors' styles and personalities were maintained. Every word was equally inspired.

Because God inspired the Bible, it is, therefore, both inerrant (without error) and infallible (incapable of error) (Matt. 5:18; John 10:35). Understanding these truths leads inevitably to the doctrine of the sufficiency of Scripture as the authority for the Christian. Mack summarizes this point well:

> The inerrancy of Scripture and the authority of Scripture are like Siamese twins—they are inseparably joined to each other. Holy Scripture, being God's law and testimony, is true and should therefore serve as our standard for all matters of faith and practice (Isa. 8:19-20). God's Word, being both truthful (John 17:17) and authoritative, calls us to humble and faithful obedience in every area of which it speaks. There is no authority that is higher than that in Scripture. Wherever and on whatever subject the Scriptures speak, one must regard them as both inerrant and authoritative.[2]

---

[2] Wayne A. Mack, "The Sufficiency of Scripture in Counseling," *Master's Seminary Journal* 9, 1 (Spring 1998), 63-64.

The key text that teaches this important doctrine is 2 Timothy 3:16–17: "All Scripture is given by inspiration of God, and is profitable for doctrine, for reproof, for correction, for instruction in righteousness, that the man of God may be complete, thoroughly equipped for every good work."

The Reformers were among the first to articulate a formulated definition of *Sola Scriptura*. They rejected the Roman Catholic notion that the church held equal authority with the Bible over doctrine and practice. As Montgomery notes,

> The Reformation irrevocably stated its theological claims upon a totally reliable, perspicuous Bible; it explicitly denied the notion of a living Magisterium as interpreter of Scripture. Indeed, the Reformers categorically refused to allow any human writing or teacher to stand above Holy Writ; they recognized fully well that if God's Word were not entirely trustworthy, then man would be forever incapable of distinguishing its truth from its non-truth and even the salvatory Gospel would be imperiled.[3]

Instead, Reformers like Martin Luther insisted that the Bible alone serves as the Christian's rule. He stated, "There was no higher authority in the church than God's Word, specifically on doctrines and teaching."[4]

An issue that rises naturally out of belief in *Sola Scriptura* is how believers are to formulate biblical ethics; that is, how to live in accordance with the moral will of God. For example, while Protestants have traditionally affirmed the sole authority of the Scriptures over both doctrine and practice, many have limited

---

[3] John Warwick Montgomery, "The Approach of New Shape Roman Catholicism to Scriptural Inerrancy: A Case Study for Evangelicals,": *Journal of the Evangelical Theological Society* 10, 4 (Fall 1967), 222.

[4] Eugene F. Klug, "Word and Scripture in Luther Studies Since World War II," *Trinity Journal* 5, 1 (Spring 1984), 3.

its authority only to those issues to which it directly speaks. Everything else that the Bible does not explicitly address is considered *adiaphora* (Greek, "things indifferent"). Music, in particular, is one of these matters that many believers consider indifferent. But, does this fit with the biblical model?

Positions on Biblical Application

Generally, approaches to the Bible's applicability to life fall into two categories. Some deny that the Bible can be applied to contemporary moral situations with any real authority, and yet others insist that as long as the Bible is interpreted and applied correctly, authoritative ethical standards may be formulated even for issues not explicitly addressed in Scripture.

Position One: An Encyclopedic View of Scripture

Some argue that if the Bible does not address a particular moral issue, believers have complete liberty to do as they please. In other words, absence of biblical directive implies moral neutrality. If God had an opinion on a particular issue, they argue, He would have given His people instructions. Rather, morally neutral actions matter only with regard to the subjective motive or conscience of the individual.

Proponents of this view often appeal to Romans 14 and 1 Corinthians 8-10 and insist that anything not explicitly addressed in Scripture falls under the principles of Christian liberty set forth in these passages. For instance, Murray argues that those who develop authoritative moral standards in apparent *adiaphora* "confuse and perplex the whole question of ethics and jeopardize the cause of truth and righteousness." He insists that unless we have the "authority of divine institution," upon a particular contemporary issue, we must not make any value judgments about it.[5] Robinson agrees when he asserts, "More heresy is preached in application than in Bible exegesis."[6] *that's true!*

Perhaps the most popular articulation of this view can be found in Charles Swindoll's *The Grace Awakening,* where he writes, "Any specified list in Scripture is to be obeyed without hesitation or question. That's an inspired list for all of us to follow, not someone's personal list. . . . But when questionable things aren't specified in Scripture, it then becomes a matter of one's personal preference or convictions."[7] *?*

Such individuals argue that this position is a correct and consistent application of *Sola Scriptura.* Belief that the Bible is sufficient for faith and practice implies that God has given His people instructions in every area He considers morally important. Childs insists that believers "recognize that at no point within the Bible is there ever spelled out a system or a technique by which one could move from the general imperatives of the law of God . . . to the specific application within the concrete situation."[8] Since believers are not given explicit instruction in certain areas, and since they are not supplied with an explicit process for applying the Bible to contemporary situations, such issues must be morally neutral.

Position Two: An Encompassing View of Scripture

Others argue that the Bible applies to all contemporary ethical situations, and authoritative standards may be formulated with issues not found in the Bible. Such standards may

---

[5] John Murray, "The Weak and the Strong," *Westminster Theological Journal* 12, 2 (May 1950), 136.
[6] Haddon Robinson, "The Heresy of Application," *Leadership Journal* 18 (Fall 1997), 21.
[7] Charles R. Swindoll, *The Grace Awakening* (Dallas: Word Publishing, 1990), 132.
[8] B. S. Childs, *Biblical Theology in Crisis* (Philadelphia: Westminster, 1976), 128.

be derived from proper application to equivalent situations. Grudem summarizes this general approach well:

> When there is no exact modern equivalent to some aspect of a command (such as, "honor the emperor" in 1 Peter 2:17), then we are still obligated to obey the command, but we do so by applying it to situations that are essentially similar to the one found in the NT. Therefore, "honor the emperor" is applied to honoring the president or the prime minister. In fact, in several such cases the immediate context contains pointers to broader applications (such as 1 Peter 2:13-14, which mentions being subject to "every human institution" including the "emperor" and "governors" as specific examples).[9]

Indeed, some would go so far as to say that proper Bible study is not finished until there is a "transferring [of] what has been learned from the text over to the waiting Church," resulting in "dynamic application of the text to one's current needs."[10]

In this view, the Bible applies to everything, even those issues not explicitly addressed in the Bible. Furthermore, those who apply the Bible correctly may authoritatively assert the moral will of God in contemporary situations. As Estes notes, "It *is* possible to claim with confidence, 'This is what the Bible says to today's situation.'" Christians today "can articulate what the passage *means* today"[11] (emphasis original).

[9] Wayne Grudem, "Review Article: Should We Move Beyond the New Testament to a Better Ethic?" *Journal of the Evangelical Theological Society* 47, 2 (June 2004), 302-303.

[10] Grant R. Osborne, *The Hermeneutical Spiral: A Comprehensive Introduction to Biblical Interpretation*, 2nd Ed. (Downers Grove, Ill.: InterVarsity Press, 2006), 410; Walter C. Kaiser, *Toward an Exegetical Theology: Biblical Exegesis for Preaching and Teaching* (Grand Rapids: Baker Book House, 1981), 149.

[11] Daniel J. Estes, "Audience Analysis and Validity in Application," *Bibliotheca Sacra* 150, 598 (April 1993), 229.

Critique of the Encyclopedic View of Scripture

Those who promote the encyclopedic view of Scripture in terms of its applicability fail to understand several key principles with regard to *Sola Scriptura* and the Bible's own example of moral application.

Sola Scriptura Understood Correctly

First, it is important to recognize that the formulators of the principle of *Sola Scriptura* never intended it to be applied in the manner of the encyclopedic view. For instance, consider these lines from Article VI of the Westminster Confession of Faith:

> The whole counsel of God, concerning all things necessary for his own glory, man's salvation, faith, and life, is either expressly set down in Scripture, *or by good and necessary consequence may be deduced from Scripture*: unto which nothing at any time is to be added, whether by new revelations of the Spirit, or traditions of men.[12]

Defenders of *Sola Scriptura* in the past realized that God intends all believers to deduce principles from His Word and apply them to every area of practice. What Luther and the other Reformers intended with *Sola Scriptura* is that the Bible must be the supreme *authority* for the Christian, <u>not</u> that it will be the <u>only source</u> of *information* utilized in the application of its authoritative principles. They recognized the necessity of using common sense and reason to apply Scripture's principles to life. As Klug notes, "Closely tied to Luther's basic principle that *Scriptura sui ipsius interpres* is the ministerial use of reason, not the abnegation of it."[13]

---

[12] James E. Bordwine, *A Guide to the Westminster Confession of Faith and Larger Catechism* (Jefferson, Mass.: The Trinity Foundation, 1991), 5-6 (emphasis added).
[13] Klug, 35.

In truth, the principle of *Sola Scriptura*, rightly understood in light of the Bible's own statements, implies that Scripture must be applied to all of life, including contemporary situations the biblical authors would have never anticipated. The principle's own primary support text, 2 Timothy 3:16-17, explicitly states this. All Scripture is profitable in such a way that the people of God can be thoroughly equipped for every good work. The word, "profitable" (Greek, *ophelimos*) communicates the idea of being beneficial, productive, and sufficient. These verses affirm the absolute sufficiency of Scripture to meet all the spiritual needs of God's people. The Bible provides the instruction to equip God's people for every good work so they are able to meet all demands of righteousness, even within contemporary contexts.

Adiaphora Understood Correctly

Promoters of the encyclopedic view of Scripture also demonstrate a misunderstanding of *adiaphora* ("things indifferent"). The formulation of the doctrine of *adiaphora* arose from within Lutheran controversy shortly after Luther's death. Some Lutherans, including Melanchthon, compromised with Rome in order to stay the rising persecution against them. In the *Leipzig Interim* (1548), Melanchthon and other Lutheran leaders compromised with Rome, not in essential doctrine, but in ceremonial requirements. They required Lutherans to submit to confirmation, episcopal ordination, extreme unction, fasts, processions, and the use of icons.

This action, which Schaff calls Melanchthon's "greatest mistake in his life,"[14] caused quite a controversy within Lutheranism. This, along with other significant controversies,

---

[14] Phillip Schaff, *The Creeds of Christendom*, Vol. I (Grand Rapids: Baker Books, 2007), 300.

led to the development of the Formula of Concord (1577), in which the doctrine of *adiaphora* was first stated. In Article X, "Of Ecclesiastical Ceremonies, Which are commonly called Adiaphora, or things indifferent," the Formula answered the question of

> whether in time of persecution and a case of confession (even though our adversaries will not agree with us in doctrine), nevertheless with a safe conscience, certain ceremonies already abrogated, which are of themselves indifferent, and neither commanded nor forbidden by God, may, on the urgent demand of our adversaries, again be re-established in use, and whether we can in this way rightly conform with the Papists in ceremonies and *adiaphora* of this sort.[15]

The conclusion of the Formula was that they "ought not yield to the enemies of the Gospel in things indifferent."[16] Instead, they should affirm liberty of conscience in such areas.

In other words, the doctrine of *adiaphora* applies specifically to requiring certain rites or ceremonies of God's people when they have not been commanded by God in Scripture. In this way, the doctrine of *adiaphora* correctly reflects the original intent of Paul's instructions in Romans 14 concerning Christian liberty — no man should be constrained to participate in a religious ceremony that has no biblical warrant. Therefore, neither the doctrine of *adiaphora* nor Christian liberty applies to decisions regarding contemporary moral situations. They apply only in situations where authorities within the Church require God's people to participate in extrabiblical religious rites.

---

[15] Ibid., Vol. III, 161.
[16] Ibid., 162.

Biblical Application Understood Correctly

The Bible's own example contradicts the encyclopedic view. The Bible does not present itself as an encyclopedia of prohibitions or as a rulebook. Pettegrew notes, "The Bible is not written to be an ethical textbook, systematically dealing with every legal, social, and ethical problem that can be imagined."[17] Instead, as Klein, Blomberg, and Hubbard note, Scripture expects its readers to correctly apply its principles to contemporary issues. They give two reasons for this view: "First, the Scriptures themselves repeatedly claim that people glorify God by obeying—that is by applying—his Word," and "Second, the Bible claims that its message is relevant for later generations, not just its original readers."[18]

Makujina also finds problems with an encyclopedic view of Scriptural moral application.[19] He specifically cites two passages that contradict such a position: Galatians 5:19-21 and Hebrews 5:11-14. He points out the phrase "and things like these" in the Galatians passage, and asserts, "Paul expected his readers to exercise intelligence and discernment in determining additional attitudes, activities, and behaviors that were similar to these."[20] In other words, Paul himself did not intend for his vice lists to be taken as encyclopedic moral prohibitions. In fact, as Makujina notes, Paul expected such "works of the flesh" as he listed to be obvious. Makujina goes so far as to argue, "Even if this already representative inventory of fifteen vices were omitted

---

[17] Larry Pettegrew, "Theological Basis of Ethics," *Master's Theological Journal* ll, 2 (Fall, 2000), 151.

[18] William W. Klein, Craig L. Blomberg, Robert L. Hubbard, eds., *Introduction to Biblical Interpretation* (Dallas: Word Publishing, 1993), 402.

[19] John Makujina, "Forgotten Texts and Doctrines in Current Evangelical Responses to Culture," presented at the East Region Annual Conference of The Evangelical Theological Society, March 26, 2004.

[20] Ibid., 4.

from Scripture, we would still be able to identify these behaviors as sinful, for they are 'obvious.'"[21]

Makujina uses the Hebrews passage to critique an encyclopedic view of biblical application. He notes that spiritual infants are those who "lack experience and skill in gleaning moral guidance from Scripture."[22] Mature Christians are those who have "trained themselves to distinguish good from evil."

Indeed, the mature advance beyond the basic teachings of the Christian faith—both doctrinal and moral—and are able to use them to make comparisons, weigh evidences, detect similarities, identify and apply principles, discern intentions, navigate through the complexities of culture-specific activities, and draw more sophisticated conclusions on the appropriateness of various behaviors and customs. But the immature are restricted to the basic teachings of right and wrong available in special revelation.[23]

The Bible itself employs this kind of methodology in application. For instance, the reason homosexuality is considered a sin in Romans 1:26–27 is that it is "unnatural." In other words, an explicit prohibition against homosexuality would not be necessary if one would simply compare the act with natural principles set forth in the creation narrative. Another similar example may be found in 1 Corinthians 11:8-9, where Paul reveals the principle behind his instructions regarding man's headship over women: "For man is not from woman, but woman from man. Nor was man created for the woman, but woman for the man."

huh ?

---

[21] Ibid.
[22] Ibid., 6.
[23] Ibid.

In summary, a proper understanding of both the principle of *Sola Scriptura* and the Bible's own example contradict an encyclopedic view of scriptural application. Indeed, proponents of such a view break their own rule, for to insist that believers *must not* apply Scripture to supposed *adiaphora* is an ethical statement with no explicit biblical warrant.

Methodology for the Encompassing View of Scripture

If the encompassing position of biblical application is correct, how, then, may a believer make accurate, authoritative applications of the Bible to contemporary circumstances? Such an endeavor is no easy task. Kaiser notes this problem when he asks, "Who has mapped out the route between these two points whereby we can move from the text of Scripture to where there is a proclamation of that text?"[24] Certainly there is no foolproof method for correct biblical interpretation but it is, nonetheless, critical to right living. Indeed, all Christians, and especially pastors, must have a basic methodology for correctly applying the Bible to their lives. Ralston summarizes what is necessary in such an endeavor: "A good Bible student must be able to identify the differences between the world of the text and the world of the audience and then build a bridge between the two worlds so that the message heard by its original audience is heard by the new audience with all of the same authority and implications."[25]

---

[24] Walter C. Kaiser, *Toward an Exegetical Theology: Biblical Exegesis for Preaching and Teaching* (Grand Rapids: Baker Book House, 1981), 18.

[25] Timothy J. Ralston, "Showing the Relevance: Application, Ethics, and Preaching," in Bock, Darrell L. and Buist M. Fanning, *Interpreting the New Testament Text: Introduction to the Art and Science of Exegesis* (Wheaton: Crossway Books, 2006), 295.

Since only the Bible carries the weight of supreme authority for a Christian, application may be authoritative only when
it is done correctly. How do we know?

Principlize

The first step in discerning how a particular passage applies to contemporary situations is to principlize its content.
Kaiser defines this step:

> To "principlize" is to state an author's propositions, argu-
> ments, narrations, and illustrations in timeless abiding
> truths with special focus on the application of those truths
> to the current needs of the Church. Contemporary appli-
> cations will often be suggested by analogous applications
> made by the original writer of the Biblical text.[26]

In doing so, the Bible student is discerning what universal
moral principles lie beneath the particular injunctions in the
passage. This is especially necessary when the injunctions are
rooted in the unique cultural circumstances of the original audience. When the believer determines the principles underneath
the cultural injunctions, as Warren explains, "specific contextu-
alizations are eliminated and specific behaviors generalized."[27]

The goal of principlizing is the discovery of universal moral absolutes rooted in the nature of God and not connected
to any particular cultural context. These may be discovered
through what Tiessen describes as "the use of good hermeneutical and exegetical procedures."[28] He argues that the dis-

---

[26] Kaiser, 152.

[27] Timothy S. Warren, "The Theological Process in Sermon Preparation," *Bibliotheca Sacra* 156, 623 (July 1999), 346.

[28] Terrance Tiessen, "Toward a Hermeneutic for Discerning Universal Moral Absolutes," *Journal of the Evangelical Theological Society* 36, 2 (June 1993), 191.

covery of such "universal and supratemporal moral norms" is certain. First, "morality is based on the unchanging nature of God." Second, "all people [are] alike in fundamental ways that are more significant than the cultural variations that differentiate them" because of the "shared human nature, created in God's image." Third, recipients of God's moral instructions possessed sinful inclinations "that continue to be true of all human beings in whatever culture."[29]

Tiessen then lists five general principles for finding universal moral absolutes: Universal norms are identifiable by (1) their basis in the moral nature of God, (2) their basis in the creation order, (3) transcendent factors in the situation of their promulgation and by the lack of situational limitation in their formulation, (4) their consistency throughout the progressive revelation of the divine will, and (5) their consistency with the progress of God's redemptive program.[30] Furthermore, Pettegrew lists five ways in which the Bible can give ethical direction: (1) prohibition, (2) permission, (3) commands, (4) precedent, and (5) example.[31] These kinds of considerations should drive the expositor's principlizing.

It is important to remember, however, that principlizing does not deny obedience to explicit commands as well. In other words, believers must obey explicit commands *and* apply the principles beneath them to contemporary situations. Proponents of the encyclopedic view limit application to the former, while some liberals limit application to the latter. But as McQuilkin and Mullen explain, to apply principles without obedience to the explicit commands is to deny the authority of Scripture.

---

[29] Ibid.
[30] Ibid., 193–203.
[31] Pettegrew, 151.

Since the Bible is the only divinely authorized word we have from God, it must be treated as the final authority. If I accept only what I discern as the principle behind a teaching, or affirm the substance of a teaching while rejecting the form, or if I set aside as normative for contemporary obedience all teaching except what can be demonstrated to be based on the nature of God, the order of creation, a universally recognized cultural phenomenon, or my theological system, my judgment supersedes the authority of the written Word. Of course many of these ways of looking at Scripture are valuable. They are valuable positively but not negatively. They are valid to help determine the meaning the Author intended, valid to reinforce the truth expressed in the text, but not valid for setting it aside. If I evaluate by criteria not authorized in Scripture what to accept and what to reject, I become the authority superior to the text itself.[32]

Extrabiblical Considerations

Once a student of the Bible has determined the principles underlying a particular text, his next step in correctly applying the text to contemporary situations is to consider information relevant to the contemporary issue. As Osborne explains, "Before we can properly apply any biblical statement to our culture or another, we must seek a deeper understanding of the specific cultural environment."[33] Klein, Blomberg, and Hubbard go so far as to say, "Faithful application of the Bible to new context requires that we become as earnest in

---

[32] McQuilkin, J. Robertson and Bradford Mullen, "The Impact of Postmodern Thinking on Evangelical Hermeneutics," *Journal of the Evangelical Theological Society* 40, 1 (March 1997), 78.

[33] Osborne, 454.

our study of the contemporary world as we are of Scripture itself."[34] Since the expositor cannot be an expert in every discipline, he must often "interact at a serious level with those disciplines and thinkers that analyze the situations into which God's Word speaks" to help him understand how universal moral principles may apply to the issue.[35] Much of this book is an attempt to investigate the other information necessary to apply the Bible's principles to music.

Those who favor the encyclopedic view and are afraid that such interaction with extrabiblical information endangers the doctrine of *Sola Scriptura* must remember that the doctrine refers to *authority* and not to *information*. Second Timothy 3:16-17 says that the Scripture is profitable for all of life, but it does not prohibit the use of additional information to understand the issue over which the believer is attempting to apply the Bible's authority. Indeed, the skeptic who insists that nothing but the Bible be used in establishing moral norms must remember, as Maddox notes,

"The very use of language is by definition a first order [extrabiblical] critical skill necessary for interpreting [and applying] Scripture."[36]

On the other hand, one must remember that even when using extrabiblical information in an attempt to understand contemporary situations, ultimately the Bible retains the right to reinterpret the information. Frame makes this point well:

It is important both to distinguish and to recognize the important relations between Scripture itself and the extrascriptural data to which we seek to apply biblical principles.

---

[34] Klein et al., 425.

[35] Dennis E. Johnson, "Spiritual Antithesis: Common Grace, And Practical Theology," *Westminster Theological Journal* 64, 1 (Spring 2002), 92.

[36] T. D. F. Maddox, "Scripture, Perspicuity, and Postmodernity," *Review and Expositor* 100, 4 (Fall 2003), 572.

Scripture is something different from extrabiblical data. But what we know of the extrabiblical data, we know by scriptural principles, scriptural norms, and the permission of Scripture. In one sense, then, all of our knowledge is scriptural knowledge. In everything we know, we know scripture. To confess anything as true is to acknowledge a biblical requirement upon us. In that sense, although there is extrabiblical data, there is no extrabiblical knowledge. All knowledge is knowledge of what Scripture requires of us.[37]

Application

The final step toward correct application of biblical principles is the application itself. Since the Bible is sufficient as an authority for all of life, the believer must strive to apply its principles even to situations not directly addressed within the pages of Scripture. When studying any passage of Scripture, the believer must ask, "What would the original author say to contemporary situations?"[38] He must correlate extrabiblical information about the contemporary issue and let the Bible's universal moral principles determine his stance toward that issue. This will be my goal regarding music in this book.

Test Case: Abortion

One example of such a process that even proponents of the encyclopedic view practice is with the issue of abortion. Few, if any, conservative Christians would defend the practice of abortion. They insist that abortion is murder. But do they find explicit statements within Scripture condemning it as

---

[37] John M. Frame, "In Defense of Something Close to Biblicism: Reflections On Sola Scriptura and History in Theological Method," *Westminster Theological Journal* 59, 2 (Fall 1997), 273.

[38] See Osborne, 441.

murder? They may reply that the killing of a human being is always murder. However, where does the Bible explicitly state that unborn infants are human beings? Furthermore, is all killing murder?

To arrive at the conclusion that abortion is morally wrong, conservative Christians—even those who hold strictly to an encyclopedic view of biblical application—must use implication, extrapolation, and consult extrabiblical information to arrive at their conclusion. The biblical principle is clear: Killing an innocent human being is sin (Ex. 20:13). But in order to bridge the gap between that principle and the conclusion that abortion is morally evil, one must employ the second step in correct application, which involves information other than explicit statements from the Bible. Grisanti lists such second-step implications from Scripture: "because [the Bible] does not distinguish between a person's state before and after birth, because it indicates God 'knew' certain ones before birth, because it indicates King David was a sinner from conception, and because John the Baptist reacted while still in his mother's womb."[39] Arriving at the conclusion that unborn infants are humans is certainly sound logic, but it is derived from extrabiblical inference rather than explicit statements. As Richard notes,

> The use of Luke 1:44 as a verse against abortion is a case in point. The statement "the baby leaped in my womb for joy" has as its *implication* the messianic divine character of Christ. An *extrapolation* is that babies in wombs have already started living before birth. It is extremely difficult to prove that this was what the human author consciously intended

[39] Michael A. Grisanti, "The Abortion Dilemma," *Master's Theological Journal* 11, 2 (Fall, 2000), 169.

[handwritten: Should we build cases on what the author probably did not intend? seems contradictory if we work so hard to figure out original intent + apply it today.]

as he penned those words. But since this extrapolation is not contrary to the statement in the verse, it may be valid as a theologicalethical [sic] extrapolate. Of course less prominent does not mean less important[40] (emphasis original).

In other words, abortion, like music, is a contemporary moral issue about which the Bible has no explicit instruction. Using sound logic and possibly extrabiblical data, a believer should come to the conclusion that unborn infants are human beings. That information combined with the universal moral principle that murder is sin should drive him to an authoritative moral principle that killing unborn infants is sin. This is the process that should be employed with all contemporary moral issues, including what music is appropriate for Christians.

Conclusion

The Bible is sufficient as the supreme authority in all areas of the Christian life. Christians are required to obey its explicit commands and all applications drawn from implication and correctly applied to a contemporary situation. This assumes, of course, that the application is valid, and in this point there is room for debate and disagreement. Disagreement with regard to the process of application to contemporary life is a futile exercise for one who is ignorant of biblical pattern, but debate over the validity of particular applications is certainly warranted and necessary.

---

[40] Ramesh P. Richard, "Methodological Proposals for Scripture Relevance: Part 2: Levels of Biblical Meaning," *Bibliotheca Sacra* 143, 570 (April 1986), 130.

Levels of Authority

The respective level of authority in applications derived from implication or extrabiblical information depends upon three factors. First, those applications more closely connected to the original intent of a text carry more authority than others. Ralston notes, "Not all applications have equal textual justification and, therefore, equal authority."[41] Second, applications may be considered authoritative only when they come from implications soundly derived from a text. Third, an application may be considered authoritative only when extrabiblical information about that given issue has been correctly understood. An ethical standard is as authoritative as explicit biblical commands when that standard is rightly understood as a sound application of a biblical, universal moral principle to a contemporary situation.

Consistent Application of *Sola Scriptura*

With these conclusions in mind, a proper understanding and application of *Sola Scriptura* implies that there is actually no such thing as *adiaphora*. As Frame notes, "From a viewpoint governed by *sola Scriptura*, the 'scope' of Scripture, the range of subject matter to which it may be applied, is unlimited."[42] He correctly argues elsewhere,

> This means that all human actions are ruled by divine commandments. There is no neutral area where God permits us to be our own lawgivers. There is no area of human life where God abdicates his rule, or where his word to us is silent. What law governs the buying of cabbage?

---

[41] Ralston, 298.
[42] Frame, "Biblicism," 274.

Well, 1 Cor. 10:31 at least, not to mention narrower biblical principles requiring parents to nourish their children, to guard the health of themselves and others, etc. Actions in accord with these biblical principles are right, actions not in accord with them are wrong. It is not a matter of merely avoiding explicit prohibitions; rather it is a matter of keeping the commands of God.[43]

Indeed, anyone who claims to hold to the sufficiency of Scripture for faith and practice must be willing to apply the Bible's principles to every situation whether or not that situation is explicitly addressed in the pages of the Bible. To fail to do so is to deny the profitability of the Word of God. As Ralston admonishes, "If the apostle Paul taught the universal profitability of the Scriptures for Christian ethics (2 Tim. 3:16-17) and the danger of information without action (1 Cor. 8:1), then those who ignore this final interpretive task encourage spiritual dysfunction. Ultimately, they have failed in the ministry of the Word."[44]

That is the task of this book. It is my desire to search the Scriptures diligently and ascertain, in the words of the Westminster Confession, the "general rules of the Word" that might be applied "by the light of nature and Christian prudence" to a discussion of music and worship in the Christian life. I desire to gather pertinent information about music by which it can be judged worthy of such biblical principles and strive to come to God-pleasing conclusions. The Bible does not explicitly lay out instructions for Christians regard-

---

[43] John M. Frame, "Some Questions about the Regulative Principle," *Westminster Theological Journal* 54, 2 (Fall 1992), 362. While I do not agree with Frame's conclusions regarding the regulative principle of worship in this essay, his argument in this statement is correct.

[44] Ralston, 293.

ing their music. But since Scripture is indeed sufficient for *all* faith and practice, so it is sufficient to help Christians determine how they should view music in their lives.

For Discussion

1. Define *Sola Scriptura*.

2. Describe several situations in the Christian life that require sources of information other than the Bible to make wise decisions.

3. How important do you consider personal Bible study in your own development? In what ways can you improve in this area?

4. Discuss several moral issues about which you hold strong convictions based on implications from the Bible rather than explicit commands.

5. List principles from the Bible that may have bearing upon a believer's understanding of what constitutes God-pleasing music.

CHAPTER TWO

What is Worship?

What worship style do you use? Do you prefer traditional or contemporary worship? Is worship for you or for God?

These questions and many more like them are prevalent in evangelical circles. Professing believers of various nationalities, denominations, and associations have begun asking the question, "What is worship?" Is worship the rituals and liturgies we find in the Old Testament? Is worship what goes on during a Sunday morning church service? Do I worship when I mow the lawn? Can I worship God by myself? Is worship even necessary today?

Godly men throughout history have tried to define worship:

Worship is *the work of acknowledging the greatness of our covenant Lord* (John Frame)[1] (emphasis original).

Worship is the believers' response of all that they are—mind, emotions, will, and body—to what God is and says and does (Warren Wiersbe).[2]

---

[1] John M. Frame, *Worship in Spirit and Truth* (Phillipsburg, N.J.: P&R Publishing, 1996), 1.

[2] Warren W. Wiersbe, *Real Worship* (Grand Rapids: Baker, 2000), 26.

To worship Jesus Christ is to attribute worth to Him (Joseph Carroll).[3]

The worship of the church, then, consists of individual, corporate, public, and private service for the Lord which is generated by a reverence for a submission to Him who is totally worthy (Charles Ryrie).[4]

Worship is to feel in the heart . . . Real worship is, among other things, a feeling about the Lord our God (A.W. Tozer).[5]

Worship is our innermost being responding with praise for all that God is, through our attitudes, actions, thoughts, and words, based on the truth of God as He has revealed Himself (John MacArthur).[6]

Worship is the activity of glorifying God in his presence with our voices and hearts (Wayne Grudem).[7]

All the controversy over what worship really is has driven believers to ask this very important question—What is worship? It is very important that we develop a sound, biblical definition of what it means to worship. To do so, we must go to the Scriptures. Any definition we contrive is insufficient unless it finds its basis in the Word of God.

Worship in the Old Testament

The most common word for worship in the Old Testament is *shachah*. Lexicons define this word: "to bow down, prostrate

---

[3] Joseph S. Carroll, *How To Worship Jesus Christ* (Chicago: Moody, 1984), 36.

[4] Charles C. Ryrie, *Basic Theology* (Wheaton: Victor, 1988), 428.

[5] A. W. Tozer, *Whatever Happened to Worship?* (Camp Hill, Pa.: Christian Publications, 1985), 82.

[6] John MacArthur Jr., *The Ultimate Priority* (Chicago: Moody, 1983), 127.

[7] Wayne Grudem, *Systematic Theology*, 1006.

oneself." In the New American Standard Bible, it is translated as "worship" 99 times, "bow" 31 times, "bow down" 18 times, "reverence" 5 times, and "fall down" 3 times. The general idea, therefore, is some kind of physical prostration in awe and reverence of someone or something. This meaning is demonstrated in several passages.

> And Jehoshaphat bowed his head with his face to the ground, and all Judah and the inhabitants of Jerusalem fell before the LORD, worshiping [shachah] the LORD (2 Chron. 20:18).

> And Ezra blessed the LORD, the great God. Then all the people answered, "Amen, Amen!" while lifting up their hands. And they bowed their heads and worshiped [shachah] the LORD with their faces to the ground (Neh. 8:6).

> Then Job arose, tore his robe, and shaved his head; and he fell to the ground and worshiped [shachah] (Job 1:20).

> Oh come, let us worship [shachah] and bow down; Let us kneel before the LORD our Maker (Ps. 95:6).

In all of these instances, *shachah* is translated with a description of physical bowing or prostration. This comprises the most common concept of worship in the Old Testament—a physical response to something. A review of the passages listed above will emphasize the reason for the response.

In 2 Chronicles 20:18, Jehoshaphat and the people fell down in worship before the Lord because of the message they had received from Him:

> Then the Spirit of the LORD came upon Jahaziel the son of Zechariah, the son of Benaiah, the son of Jeiel, the son of Mattaniah, a Levite of the sons of Asaph, in the midst of

the assembly. And he said, "Listen, all you of Judah and you inhabitants of Jerusalem, and you, King Jehoshaphat! Thus says the LORD to you: 'Do not be afraid nor dismayed because of this great multitude, for the battle is not yours, but God's. Tomorrow go down against them. They will surely come up by the Ascent of Ziz, and you will find them at the end of the brook before the Wilderness of Jeruel. You will not need to fight in this battle. Position yourselves, stand still and see the salvation of the LORD, who is with you, O Judah and Jerusalem!' Do not fear or be dismayed; tomorrow go out against them, for the LORD is with you" (2 Chron. 20:14-17).

The people bowed down and worshiped the Lord in Nehemiah 8:6 because they had heard His Word read to them:

Now all the people gathered together as one man in the open square that was in front of the Water Gate; and they told Ezra the scribe to bring the Book of the Law of Moses, which the LORD had commanded Israel. So Ezra the priest brought the Law before the assembly of men and women and all who could hear with understanding on the first day of the seventh month. Then he read from it in the open square that was in front of the Water Gate from morning until midday, before the men and women and those who could understand; and the ears of all the people were attentive to the Book of the Law (Neh. 8:1-3).

Job fell to the ground in worship after news of his family's death. His response was to trust and depend on the sovereign control of God over the situation. The reason for the command to bow down in worship in Psalm 95 is also clear. "Oh come, let us worship and bow down; Let us kneel before the LORD our Maker. For He is our God, And we are the people of His pasture, And the sheep of His hand" (Psalm 95:6-7).

In every instance, the physical response of worship relates directly to an understanding of truth about God. In 2 Chronicles 20 the people realized the Lord was going to protect them. In Nehemiah the people heard truth from His Word. Job responded with dependence on God's sovereignty even during a difficult trial.

When we consider worship in the Old Testament, we often think of the physical manifestations of worship—the rituals, the bowing, the sacrifices, and so forth. Authors, who are attempting to define worship biblically, often do so in those kinds of terms. However, if we examine the essential essence of worship in these biblical references, it is clear that no matter what form worship took, in the Old Testament it consisted primarily of two elements *a presentation of truth about God and a fitting response to that truth.* No matter if the worship was expressed actively through ritual and ceremony or if it was a spontaneous reaction, the essence of the worship was the same—response to truth about God.

Worship in the New Testament

In the Septuagint (the Greek translation of the Old Testament), *shachah* is translated with the word *proskuneo*, which means virtually the same as its Hebraic counterpart. It emphasizes a physical manifestation of worship. *Proskuneo* is common in the Gospels (26 occurrences). People would often bow

Why don't we emphasize a physical response?

down worshipfully before Jesus when they understood who He really was. For example, "And as they went to tell His disciples, behold, Jesus met them, saying, 'Rejoice!' So they came and held Him by the feet and worshiped Him" (Matt. 28:9).

This word is also common in the book of Revelation (21 times) because the angels and elders in heaven often bow down before God because of who He is. "The twenty-four elders fall down before Him who sits on the throne and worship Him who lives forever and ever" (Rev. 4:10).

So in the Gospels and Revelation, the concept of worship is very similar to the Old Testament. Worship is a response (often physical) to an understanding of truth about God.

It is interesting that *proskuneo* virtually disappears in Acts and the Epistles, which is why we cannot tie the essence of worship to some kind of outward physical description. The word that replaces *proskuneo* in these books is *latreuo*, which is usually translated "serve."

> For God is my witness, whom I serve [*latreuo*] with my spirit in the gospel of His Son, that without ceasing I make mention of you always in my prayers (Rom. 1:9).

> I beseech you therefore, brethren, by the mercies of God, that you present your bodies a living sacrifice, holy, acceptable to God, which is your reasonable service [*latreuo*] (Rom. 12:1).

> For we are the circumcision, who worship [*latreuo*] God in the Spirit, rejoice in Christ Jesus, and have no confidence in the flesh (Phil. 3:3).

Paul de-emphasizes the physical manifestations of worship, which helps us recognize its essential element, a response to truth about God. For instance, the "therefore" in Romans

12:1 demonstrates that offering our bodies as sacrifices of worship is in response to the rich truths laid out in chapters 1-11. Notice also *latreuo* is often connected with an emphasis upon the internal spirit of man, such as in Romans 1:9 and Philippians 3:3.

The Essence of Worship

Christ emphasized this essential definition of worship in His discussion with the Samaritan woman in John 4. When Jesus met the woman at the well and confronted her about her sin, she tried to change the subject, and in doing so, provided Christ the opportunity to address the very important topic of worship. The woman asked Jesus what the proper means of worshiping was:

> Jesus said to her, "Woman, believe Me, the hour is coming when you will neither on this mountain, nor in Jerusalem, worship the Father. You worship what you do not know; we know what we worship, for salvation is of the Jews. But the hour is coming, and now is, when the true worshipers will worship the Father in spirit and truth; for the Father is seeking such to worship Him. God is Spirit, and those who worship Him must worship in spirit and truth" (John 4:21-24).

Because of God's strict commands concerning worship, the Jews at that time were very concerned with the outward forms—where, when, and how they should worship. The woman was asking what the proper outward forms of worship should be. Jesus replied that with His coming, the outward forms weren't necessary anymore, and He emphasized the two essential elements of worship, namely spiritual response (spirit) and understanding of truth.

Therefore, worship can be defined as follows: [*Worship is a spiritual response to God as a result of understanding biblical truth about God.*] This definition captures the biblical essence of worship and can be expressed in countless ways through actions, attitudes, and affections. In reality, worship should encompass all of life as we have seen especially in the language of the Epistles.

Worship in All of Life

Worship Begins with Understanding Biblical Truth about God.

Worship in Scripture always includes a presentation of truth about God. Perhaps a few more examples will be helpful.

> The LORD reigns; Let the peoples tremble! He dwells between the cherubim; Let the earth be moved! The LORD is great in Zion, And He is high above all the peoples. Let them praise Your great and awesome name—He is holy. The King's strength also loves justice; You have established equity; You have executed justice and righteousness in Jacob. Exalt the LORD our God, And worship at His footstool—He is holy (Ps. 99:1-5).

> Make a joyful shout to the LORD, all you lands! Serve the LORD with gladness; Come before His presence with singing. Know that the LORD, He is God; It is He who has made us, and not we ourselves; We are His people and the sheep

of His pasture. Enter into His gates with thanksgiving, And into His courts with praise. Be thankful to Him, and bless His name. For the LORD is good; His mercy is everlasting, And His truth endures to all generations (Ps. 100).

It is clear from these passages that the reason for the response of worship is always an understanding of truth about God. For instance, in Psalm 99 the responses of trembling, praise, and exultation are the result of understanding that God reigns and that He is holy, just, and right. In Psalm 100, responses of joy, thankfulness, and praise are the result of understanding that God is Creator and that He is good, loving, and faithful.

For worship to be directed to God, the worshiper must understand the truth about God. That is why the preaching of God's Word should be central in a worship service. It is why a believer must be studying the Word of God if he is to worship God with all of his life. Without understanding God, a person cannot worship Him. *If the Word is not central, is it truly worship? What if you can't understand the Words or they are un-biblical?*

God is known in two ways—by His character and by His works. Both are necessary in a presentation of truth about God. God's character consists of attributes that describe Him such as holiness, sovereignty, power, love, faithfulness, justice, righteousness, grace, and mercy. God's works are those things He has done to display His character. The scriptural examples above clearly indicate that God is being worshiped because of truth rooted in Himself, either who He is or what He has done. Only when God's character and works are seen can He truly be worshiped in a biblical way.

God's Word is the primary source for observing God. Scripture is full of descriptions of God's attributes as well as instances of His deeds that display those attributes. God can certainly be known through creation and through our own personal experiences, but the Bible is the only true, absolute, sure source of truth. We can very easily misinterpret our own experiences, or they can change with our circumstances and emotions, but God's Word is the one dependable source of truth. This is why the Bible must have preeminence in worship. The Bible is God's means of communicating Himself to His people.

It is not enough for worshipers to observe truth about God. They must also understand that truth. An understanding of truth includes the truth itself and all its implications for us. God means for His people to see and acknowledge His truth. That will often require careful teaching and explanation of the biblical text. Commentaries and other resources can help someone in his personal understanding, while the local church pastor provides weekly exegesis for his people.

Worship Results in Proper Spiritual Response to God.

God is not worshiped, however, when people simply see and understand the truth. A believer must also respond to that truth. The foundation of worship is not only truth about God, but it is also a response directed to God. The believer hears, understands, and accepts truth about God, and then he directs a response toward the God from whom the truth came. What does it mean to "respond" to truth from God? Let's look at some examples of responses from the Bible.

I will praise the LORD according to His righteousness: and will sing praise to the name of the LORD most high (Ps. 7:17 KJV).

Give unto the LORD the glory due unto his name: bring an offering, and come before him: worship the LORD in the beauty of holiness (1 Chron. 16:29 KJV).

Sing unto God, sing praises to his name: extol him that rideth upon the heavens by his name YAH [LORD], and rejoice before him (Ps. 68:4 KJV).

Some proper responses to truth about God are things like thanks, praise, exultation, and adoration. Other passages demonstrate responses toward God such as brokenness, contrition, and grief (Ps. 51:17; 38:18); longing and desire (Ps. 42:1-2; 73:25-26); fear and awe (Ps. 5:7; 33:8; 103:3-5); gratitude (Ps. 100:4); and joy and hope (Ps. 32:11; 42:5). God is truly glorified when His people respond to truth about Him. In what ways are these responses manifested? We respond in two ways—with our affections and with our actions.

I will explain what I mean by the term "affection" more fully in chapter 4, but for now I will just say that affection is more than sweaty palms or a quickened heartbeat. It is more than mere chemical response to some external stimulus. Affection is the internal response of our spirit to what we know, and it is what drives us to follow what we know to be true. The difference between the two is like the difference between laughing because you're being tickled and laughing because you get a joke. If someone tickles you, nothing intellectual has to occur for you to laugh. Your response of laughing is simply an involuntary physical response to a stimulus. On the other hand, if you laugh because you have just been told a joke, you are laughing as a result of something that has occurred in your intellect—you got the punch line! So when I say that we respond to truth with our affections, understand that I mean more than some kind of physical "tingle." See chapter 4 for a more thorough discussion.

Another important form of response to an understanding of truth about God is action. That connects more with the concept of worship in all of life. Our every action should be a response of worship to the Lord. These actions can take the form of obedience to explicit commands. We respond a certain way because we understand that God is holy and that He will punish sin. Responses of action can also take the form of making choices with the purpose of bringing glory to God. We will discuss later how to make those choices.

Putting all of this together, then, we arrive at our biblical definition of worship: *Worship is a spiritual response to God as a result of understanding biblical truth about God.*

Conclusion

Many Christians segment their lives into "sacred" and "secular." It is true, of course, that when believers gather for public worship or speak of biblical matters, more narrowed considerations must govern what is acceptable. However, according to our Lord's words in John 4, all of life is worship, not just what happens on Sunday mornings.

Therefore, it is incumbent upon Christians to view every decision they make in life as a decision of worship. Is the decision a correct response (of action or affection) to truth you know about God from His Word? This should motivate a believer to live an active life of progressing in holiness, an important topic we will consider in the next chapter.

For Discussion

1. Define the biblical essence of worship.

2. Discuss why understanding biblical truth about God is so important for worship.

3. What can you learn about God and His character from sources other than the Bible?

4. List several truths about God and responses that are appropriate for each truth.

CHAPTER THREE

Understanding Sanctification

The first step in deciding what is and is not appropriate for believers, including musical styles, is to understand the purpose of the Christian life. Ephesians 2:10 says of the Christian, "For we are His workmanship, created in Christ Jesus for good works, which God prepared beforehand that we should walk in them."

From this passage and others, it is clear that individuals are saved to perform good works. That is what God has ordained. Believers are to magnify Christ through their lives. Many Christians, however, are simply satisfied with mediocre Christianity. They obey explicit commands and abstain from explicit sins, but that's about it. That is not acceptable Christianity! It is not glorifying God with your whole life.

Sanctification: Actively Pursuing Godliness

Believers are positionally sanctified (set apart) from sin unto God at the moment of their salvation (1 Cor. 6:11). They are progressively sanctified from sin through the continual work of the Holy Spirit during their lifetime (Phil. 1:6). Ultimately, in the eternal kingdom, believers will be freed from the very presence of sin (1 John 3:2). However, though believers will inevitably persevere (1 Peter 1:3-4, 7), sanctification is not automatic. Believers are commanded to actively pursue holiness (Titus 2:12).

Therefore, the Bible presents a Christian's progressive sanctification as an active process in which a believer pursues godliness, proves excellent things, and puts on things that conform him to the image of Christ. He does this through the power of God working within him (Phil. 2:12-13). Sanctification is active.

> And this I pray, that your love may abound still more and more in knowledge and all discernment, that you may approve the things that are excellent, that you may be sincere and without offense till the day of Christ, being filled with the fruits of righteousness which are by Jesus Christ, to the glory and praise of God (Phil. 1:9-11).

> And have put on the new man who is renewed in knowledge according to the image of Him who created him, where there is neither Greek nor Jew, circumcised nor uncircumcised, barbarian, Scythian, slave nor free, but Christ is all and in all. Therefore, as the elect of God, holy and beloved, put on tender mercies, kindness, humility, meekness, longsuffering; bearing with one another, and forgiving one another, if anyone has a complaint against another; even as Christ forgave you, so you also must do. But above all these things put on love, which is the bond of perfection (Col. 3:10-14).

> But the wisdom that is from above is first pure, then peaceable, gentle, willing to yield, full of mercy and good fruits, without partiality and without hypocrisy. Now the fruit of righteousness is sown in peace by those who make peace (James 3:17-18).

As His divine power has given to us all things that pertain to life and godliness, through the knowledge of Him who called us by glory and virtue, by which have been given to us exceedingly great and precious promises, that through these you may be partakers of the divine nature, having escaped the corruption that is in the world through lust. But also for this very reason, giving all diligence, add to your faith virtue, to virtue knowledge, to knowledge self-control, to self-control perseverance, to perseverance godliness, to godliness brotherly kindness, and to brotherly kindness love. For if these things are yours and abound, you will be neither barren nor unfruitful in the knowledge of our Lord Jesus Christ. For he who lacks these things is shortsighted, even to blindness, and has forgotten that he was cleansed from his old sins. Therefore, brethren, be even more diligent to make your call and election sure, for if you do these things you will never stumble; for so an entrance will be supplied to you abundantly into the everlasting kingdom of our Lord and Savior Jesus Christ (2 Peter 1:3-11).

This is the biblical model for sanctification. It is a life pursuing righteousness and godly characteristics. It is striving to prove excellent and beneficial qualities.

Principles for Making Godly Decisions

In 1 Corinthians 8-10, Paul deals with a topic that was just as controversial in his time as the issue of music styles is in ours, namely, whether believers should eat meat offered to idols. Paul comes to the conclusion that he has the right to do so but will refrain for various reasons. In this section, Paul lays down some principles by which we can evaluate questionable areas in our lives.

Is It Beneficial for Sanctification?

> All things are lawful for me, but not all things are helpful;
> all things are lawful for me, but not all things edify. Let
> no one seek his own, but each one the other's well-being
> (1 Cor. 10:23-24).

Paul was so concerned with his sanctification and the
glory of God that he was willing to give up what may have
been permissible for him but not necessarily beneficial. With
regard to music and any other questionable area in the Christian life, we often ask, "What's wrong with it?" However, this
approach does not fit with a life that is actively pursuing sanctification. Instead, we should be asking, "What's right with
it?" Something may be permissible, but is it really beneficial
and edifying for yourself and others? Does it have a positive
influence? Is it helping you increase in your sanctification? Is
it drawing you closer to God?

Some sort yes

Does It Risk Failing to Bring God Glory?

> Therefore, whether you eat or drink, or whatever you do,
> do all to the glory of God (1 Cor. 10:31).

A Christian's number one concern in life should not be his
rights or his preferences. It should be the glory of God. Many
Christians see how far they can go without crossing "the line,"
yet why would a believer risk failing to bring God glory?
    If a man were in a foggy forest at night and he knew there
was quicksand somewhere down the road, he would be foolish to see how far into the fog he could go until he reached the
quicksand. And yet Christians push farther and farther every
day, seeing just how close they can get to the line and still be

What if the motive is pure & can they in it do good conscience?

40

okay. That is certainly not pleasing to the Lord regardless of whether they actually cross the line.

Why would we even want to risk displeasing the Lord? Why would we want to risk that our questionable decisions may lead us farther and farther toward the quicksand? Dedicated believers wouldn't. Only people who are more concerned with their own preferences than what God desires would risk the danger.

Does It Offend Others?

> But beware lest somehow this liberty of yours become a stumbling block to those who are weak (1 Cor. 8:9).

> Give no offense, either to the Jews or to the Greeks or to the church of God, just as I also please all men in all things, not seeking my own profit, but the profit of many, that they may be saved (1 Cor. 10:32-33).

First Corinthians 8:9 makes it clear: Biblical offense is not defined in the same way we may use it today. It does not mean that our feelings are hurt because of something done to us. On the contrary, offending someone conveys the idea of causing someone else to stumble into sin because of your actions. Paul says that he has liberty to give up what is legitimately his right if it will be a stumbling block to a weaker brother. We should be willing to give up questionable music if it could cause someone else to sin.

Does It Control Me?

> All things are lawful for me, but all things are not helpful. All things are lawful for me, but I will not be brought under the power of any (1 Cor. 6:12).

But I discipline my body and bring it into subjection, lest, when I have preached to others, I myself should become disqualified (1 Cor. 9:27).

Many people are unwilling even to discuss some questionable areas because they do not want to find out that what they like is displeasing to God. The Bible condemns that attitude. It can even take the form of sentimentality, loving something more than God does. If we are simply unwilling to give up something in our lives, then it controls us. That is all the more reason to give it up, even if it is not inherently ungodly.

making an idol

Conclusion

The bottom line is this: If you are not actively pursuing sanctification; if you are not daily in God's Word, striving to know His mind and think His thoughts; if you are not willing to give up what might be legitimately your right, then you cannot expect to discern what music styles are pleasing to the Lord.

Our job is to learn what God likes, and it is only when we are consistently in His Word and willing to do whatever it takes to pursue holiness that we will begin to think God's thoughts after Him. We should not be comfortable with mediocre Christianity. We should not be satisfied with lives filled with things that are questionable at best and that do not aid us in our Christian walk. We should be willing to give up those things to reach the goal of glorifying God and worshiping Him with our choices.

For Discussion

1. What is the difference between positional sanctification and progressive sanctification?

2. List some things that might be permissible for you, but are not profitable for your spiritual life.

3. What are some areas in your life that have the potential of causing someone else to stumble into sin?

CHAPTER FOUR

Affections–The Missing Link

As school violence, drug abuse, and premarital sex grow in
the youth culture of America, government officials and educa-
tors seem to come to the same conclusion: These problems can
be solved with more education. Provide better education on the
harmful effects of drugs, illicit sex, and violence, and America's
youth will change for the better. Yet as funding for sex education, drug awareness, and violence seminars increases, these
same problems continue to run rampant. Educating the mind,
it seems, is not enough to change the will.

The same problem exists in evangelical churches today. Sinful action seems to be on the rise, and church leaders rightly
diagnose the problem as one of doctrine–Christians do not
rightly understand God, the nature of Christianity, and their
responsibilities as followers of Christ. Yet as an emphasis on
right doctrine increases in contemporary evangelicalism, Christian living does not seem to improve.

Why is this so? If the root problem behind wrong living is
wrong thinking, why does not education of the mind directly influence the will to do what is right? There is a great missing link

between the mind and the will that we must recover if Christians are going to connect what they know to be true with how they live. There is an additional problem: An exclusive emphasis on the mind as that which influences the life leads people to insist that practical decisions like music are relative since the Bible does not deal with the subject in a systematic, doctrinal manner. However, identifying the missing link between mind and will may correct that error as well.

This missing link is emphasized throughout Scripture but perhaps nowhere more clearly than in what the Jews consider their pledge of allegiance: "Hear, O Israel: The LORD our God, the LORD is one! You shall love the LORD your God with all your heart, with all your soul, and with all your strength" (Deut. 6:4-5).

The Jews call this passage of Scripture the *shema*, the Hebrew term for the first word in the verse, "hear." They consider this text central to their religion, and even Jesus referenced it several times during His earthly ministry. The passage answers the question, "What is true religion?" In other words, what is the essence of religion that enables us to live how God wants us to live? Moses delivered the *shema* to the nation of Israel just after he brought down the Ten Commandments, and this verse summarizes all that made up the Jewish religion. As we study the passage, we must remember that those commands were given in the context of a covenant between Yahweh and Israel, but they express truths that apply to us today and to our consideration of what makes true religion. And with a little further revelation from the New Testament, we may apply its truths fully to Christianity.

True Religion Begins with Certain Affirmations.

The Jewish pledge of allegiance begins with a requirement to believe certain things in order to be religious. There are certain facts that each person must accept to ascribe to biblical religion. The first of these affirmations is that Yahweh is our God. Yahweh, the Hebrew name for God that distinguishes Him from all other pagan gods, means, "to exist." And so the first affirmation that defines true religion is that Yahweh, the God of the Bible, is our God. Not Baal, Buddha, or Allah; Yahweh, the God of the Bible, is our God.

But then Moses slaps on a further qualification. Not only is Yahweh *our* God, Yahweh is the *only* God. There is one true and living God. In other words, only one being in the entire universe genuinely deserves to be worshiped. The one true God is Yahweh, the God of the Bible. Religion, first of all, begins with affirmation of the truth that there is only one God whom we will worship, and that God is Yahweh. So the second affirmation, crucial to true religion, is that this Yahweh who is our God is the one and only God.

Throughout history God has given revealed truth to man in stages, and man has been responsible to live according to whatever revelation he has from God. I mentioned earlier that the *shema* was given to Israel long ago, but it still comprises an affirmation of the central truths of biblical religion. The nation of Israel did not have the revelation of the New Testament, but we do. There is one very important truth that we must add to these affirmations that is crucial to the true *Christian* religion. In John 14:6, Jesus Christ says, "I am the way, the truth, and the life. No one comes to the Father except through Me." The reason this is the case is because Jesus is both Yahweh and man. The Bible specifically calls Jesus "Yahweh" (John 8:58, translated "I AM"). And so the third affirmation of truth crucial to true religion is this: Jesus Christ is the only way to Yahweh.

To discover the essence of true religion, we must first recognize that true religion begins with certain affirmations: (1) Yahweh is our God; (2) Yahweh is the only God; and (3) Jesus Christ is the only way to Yahweh. These affirmations are fundamental to true religion. If someone is going to please God with his life, he must believe these essential doctrinal truths and all of their implications.

True Religion Results in Certain Actions.

The second crucial point in a definition of true religion is not stated explicitly in the *shema*, but it is implied in the context of the passage and stated explicitly elsewhere in Scripture. The immediate context of this, the essential Jewish statement of biblical religion, is the giving of the law to the people of Israel. God required certain things of His people, and their adherence to those requirements demonstrated whether they were truly His spiritual children. These actions were proof of true religion. Ecclesiastes 12:13 says, "Let us hear the conclusion of the whole matter: Fear God and keep His commandments, For this is man's all."

The same is true today and is explicitly stated in the New Testament. For instance, 1 John 3:6-9:

Whoever abides in Him does not sin. Whoever sins has neither seen Him nor known Him. Little children, let no one deceive you. He who practices righteousness is righteous, just as He is righteous. He who sins is of the devil, for the devil has sinned from the beginning. For this purpose the Son of God was manifested, that He might destroy the works of the devil. Whoever has been born of God does not sin, for His seed remains in him; and he cannot sin, because he has been born of God.

And again in chapter 5, verse 18, "We know that whoever is born of God does not sin; but he who has been born of God keeps himself, and the wicked one does not touch him."

And John 15:14, "You are My friends if you do whatever I command you."

So belief in certain truths is the beginning of true religion, and true religion is proven through certain actions in obedience to God's commands. If you are religious, you will believe certain things, and you will do certain things.

Some people stop here in their reasoning. Many say that belief in Yahweh as the one and only God and in Jesus Christ, God's eternal Son, as the only way to God the Father is the essence of true religion. Others see biblical warrant for insisting that biblical belief results in biblical actions. But most people stop here. They define true religion as belief in God and obedience to His commands. Wouldn't you define religion that way? Many professing believers across the world live this way. They think true religion consists in believing the right things and acting the right way. So they do good deeds like reading the Bible, trying to do what is right, going to church, being kind to others, and trying to rear their children rightly. They try to do good and live right. In reality their view of the essence of religion is duty to God, and that is true to a certain extent. But it is not the full answer. I believe that kind of thinking—the idea that the essence of religion is simply obedience to God's commands—is a dangerous problem in our day. I think it is a serious problem for two reasons.

First, the belief that duty is the essence of true religion does not glorify God. Let me give you an illustration to demonstrate what I mean. Recently on my wife Becky's birthday, I surprised her in her classroom with some roses and cupcakes for her class.

Now suppose Becky had said, "Oh, Scott, you're so wonderful. Why are you doing all this for me?" What if I had replied, "Well, Becky, you know, we're married, and it's my duty to do nice things for you." Of course you can see how unflattering this would be to my wife. Why do we think it would be any less glorifying to God for us to live simply out of duty?[1]

The other reason that viewing religion as simply obedience to God's commands is a problem is that it is simply unbiblical. Religion does not consist of mere duty. Scripture presents an entirely different picture of true religion. We have seen that obedience to God's commands is the evidence of true religion, but it is not its biblical essence. Let's use our illustration again to help discover what the true essence of religion is. Instead of giving my wife flowers simply out of duty, I would have said, "Becky I'm doing this for you not out of duty, but because I love you, and nothing brings me more pleasure than to please you and see you happy."

You see, the essence of the relationship I have with my wife and the essence of a relationship with God is *affection*. Without deep, heartfelt affection there is no relationship. We can believe all the right things intellectually, and we can try to do all the right things, but without affection for the Lord we will not be able to do what is right. Affection is the source of right actions, because in the regular course of life we do only what we love. We may say we believe in something, and we may try to act a certain way, but if we do not love what we believe, we will not succeed.

So, while true religion begins with certain affirmations and is proven by certain actions, true religion flows from cer-

---

[1] The point of this illustration is borrowed from John Piper, *Desiring God: Meditations of a Christian Hedonist* (Sisters, Ore.: Multnomah Books, 1996).

tain affections. The *shema* bears this out: "Hear, O Israel: The
LORD our God, the LORD is one! You shall love the LORD your
God with all your heart, with all your soul, and with all your
strength" (Deut. 6:4-5). What do I love?

True Religion Flows from Certain Affections.

God commands us to have certain affections for Him,
and the greatest of these is love. Christ makes that clear when
He says the greatest commandment comes right from this passage, the shema: "Love the Lord your God with all your heart
and with all your soul and with all your mind" (Matt. 22:37
from Deut. 6:5).

It is important to understand exactly what the Lord means
when He commands us to love Him. You might ask, "Isn't it
obvious? We know what it means to love." But there are many
different kinds of love, and not all are appropriate for expression to the Lord. For instance, I love my wife, I love pizza, I
love soccer, and I love God. But I do not love each of these in
the same way, nor do I express my love in the same manner.
If I expressed love for my wife in the same way I express love
for pizza or soccer, she would be unhappy, and rightly so. Likewise, if I express love to God in the same way I express love
to my wife, He would be very displeased. We must remember
the context of this command. Love in the context of a covenant relationship is not a warm, gushy feeling in our bosom
or a tingling in our toes. [Love in the covenant relationship
involves a deeply rooted commitment of the heart and mind.]
We have been so influenced by pop culture that we no longer
understand what biblical love is.

In modern thought, emotion is generally considered neutral. The only criterion of worth for emotion is the object toward which it is expressed. This relatively novel thinking, however, must be corrected to distinguish between different qualities of emotion. Not all emotion is created equal, especially for expression to God. A man should not love his wife in the same way that he loves his dog. Additionally, there is a great difference between emotion that is merely physical feeling and emotion that involves the whole of man. Well-known theologian Jonathan Edwards differentiated between "passions" and "affections" in his treatise, *Religious Affections*:

> The affections and passions are frequently spoken of as the same, and yet in the more common use of speech, there is in some respect a difference. Affection is a word that in the ordinary signification, seems to be something more extensive than passion, being used for all vigorous lively actings of the will or inclination, but passion for those that are more sudden, and whose effects on the animal spirits are more violent, and the mind more over powered, and less in its own command.[2]

> The affections are no other than the more vigorous and sensible exercises of the inclination and will of the soul.[3]

Edwards' thinking reflects anthropological thought prior to the Enlightenment. Modern thinking sees man as comprised of mind, will, and emotion. Pre-modern thought, however, understood a distinction within the category of

---

[2] Jonathan Edwards, *Religious Affections* (Carlisle, Pa.: Banner of Truth, 2001), 26-27.
[3] Ibid., 24.

emotion between the affections and the passions, the former being a component of the will and the latter simply part of man's physiology.

"Passions" are surface-level feelings that are merely physical, chemical responses to some sort of stimulus. Blushing when embarrassed, experiencing "butterflies" in your stomach, or "goose bumps" are examples of such passionate responses. Passions include things like fear, anger, sentimentalism, sexual drive, and appetite. They are not wrong, but they are not the measure of true spiritual response to truth and should never be allowed to control us. Whenever a person is controlled by his gut, his passions, he will fail to do what is right. A man controlled by his appetite is a glutton. One controlled by anger finds himself with an uncontrollable temper. A person who allows his sexual drive to control him will fail morally.

"Affections," on the other hand, involve the mind. They arise as a result of some sort of cognitive understanding of truth. They are not immediate but developed. They are not merely surface level physical responses; they support the intellect. Affections are so important to develop because we need noble affections to keep our passions in check. Without biblical affections, passions will always win over the mind.

Again, this kind of thinking reflects the understanding of theologians prior to the Enlightenment. The affections, which were essentially associated with the soul, were considered superior to the passions, which were associated with the body. This was not a kind of Platonism that considered the body to be evil. Nevertheless, the passions were something that, in the words of Paul, we must always "bring...into subjection" (1 Cor. 9:27) lest they control us. For instance, Cooper argues that Augustine believed "the body tends to divert the soul from spiritual things and to tempt it with sinful desires."[4] On the other hand, with rationalism came a purely scientific explanation of human nature, turning man into a mere animal composed of mind, will, and body. As Tarnas explains, "The Christian dualistic stress on the supremacy of the spiritual and transcendent over the material and concrete was now largely inverted, with the physical world becoming the predominant focus for human activity."[5]

To combat our rationalism-influenced understanding of emotion and return to the biblical concept, it is important to look at the word "heart" in the *shema*. When we hear this word, we automatically think of emotions in terms of romantic or warm, fuzzy feelings. But for the original audience of this text, the word *heart* meant so much more. The word *heart* does include a concept of the emotions, but it also includes the mind and the will, the whole of man. This is why God can command us to have affections. Love in the portrayal of pop media is something we "fall into," something involuntary, even accidental. But biblical affection is not that way. Biblical affection intricately involves the mind, the will, and the emotions.

That is why biblical affection is the essence of true religion; biblical affection comes from the affirmation of right biblical truths, and it results in right actions. Without right beliefs there would be no right affection, but without right affection there would be no right action.

---

[4] John W. Cooper, *Body, Soul & Life Everlasting: Biblical Anthropology and the Monism-Dualism Debate* (Grand Rapids: Eerdmans, 1989), 10.

[5] Richard Tarnas, *The Passion of the Western Mind: Understanding the Ideas that Have Shaped Our World View* (New York: Ballantine Books, 1991), 285-286.

Obedience Flows from Right Affections.

Religious affections are the spring out of which obedience to God's commands flow. When it comes to day-to-day living, we are ruled by what we love. We may say we believe certain things, but unless we truly love them, we will not follow them. That is why true religion, in great part, consists in the affections. Anyone can believe certain facts. Anyone can do certain things. But only those who are truly regenerated, who are truly religious, will love what they believe and what they do. And from this love flows the ability to do what is right.

Let's use war as an example. Think about an American soldier on foreign soil whose job is to guard a certain road. He is serving his country because of certain beliefs that he has about his country and freedom. Now what if during his shift a band of angry insurgents comes down the road toward him? What keeps that soldier from turning and running for his life? Is it his intellectual beliefs that motivate him to stand firm and fight? In a sense, it is his beliefs. Were it not for those beliefs, he would not stand firm. However, I dare say that as the insurgents move toward him, the soldier is not thinking through his beliefs intellectually. At that moment, in the heat of battle, it is not the beliefs *per se* that are sustaining him; it is his affections. He not only believes in his country and freedom, he loves his country and freedom. It is not just intellectual assent that motivates him and sustains him. It is courage. To be honest, I believe in this country and in freedom just as much as those soldiers, but I'm not so sure I would have the courage to do what they do. Those affections take time to develop, and without them, the soldier would be overcome with fear.

You see, we can say we believe certain things, but we will *do* only what we *love*. It is affection that is at the heart of true religion. Without belief in Christ there is no salvation. But the new birth from God that engendered the faith also creates within us the affections to love and take joy in what we believe. And then when the pressures and trials of life come our way, we stand firm and our faith is proven genuine because we have a *love* for Christ and a *joy* that is inexpressible that will carry us through (1 Peter 1).

Jonathan Edwards noted that the affections and the will are not separate. He called affection the inclination of the will, that is, what inclines us to follow through with what we believe. That is really the true nature of faith. There is a kind of faith that does not save (James 2:14). It is simply intellectual assent and does not result in right living. But true, saving faith has implicit within it a love for and trust in what is believed. And this connection between what we know and what we love is what will produce a godly life.

We Must Guard Those Things that Shape Our Affections.

It is of utmost importance, therefore, that we carefully guard what shapes our affections. This is a dire need in contemporary evangelicalism. That is why I have included such a lengthy discussion of the affections in a book about music. Things that shape and govern our affections surround us: music, movies, books—all of culture molds and guides our affections. That is the whole purpose of music; music is the language of emotions. So what we listen to and those cultural activities we digest shape and form our affections either rightly or wrongly. And for this reason we must be very careful what we allow to shape our affections.

That is especially true for the affections we express to our holy God. God is not glorified when we express to Him emo-

[handwritten margin notes: Rom 12:1-2 "Don't let this world squeeze us into its mold - are we doing that w/ music."]

tions that are unworthy of Him. We are commanded to have awe for the Lord, but not the same kind of awe we express when we cherish a newborn child. We are commanded to rejoice in the Lord, but not the same kind of joy we express at a sporting event. We are commanded to adore our Lord, but not the same kind of adoration a teenage girl gives to a rock star. We are commanded to love the Lord, but not the same kind of love we express to our wives, let alone the sensual love of brothels. This concept will be elaborated in section 3.

We must grasp the fact that not all emotions are created equal. Some emotions are appropriate only for certain occasions and other emotions are never appropriate. And not all emotions are appropriate for expression to God. We must guard those expressions of affection we give to the Lord in worship and choose only those expressions that are worthy of His holy name.

But we should not stop with just expressions of affection in worship. We must remember that whatever we allow into our lives shapes our affections. Some people are very careful about the expressions of affection they give to the Lord on Sunday, but they are not so careful the rest of the week. Some people are concerned that the music chosen for a worship service expresses right affection for the Lord, but during the week they listen to music that debases their affections and makes it virtually impossible to express right affection for the Lord. No wonder we have difficulty appreciating music and other forms of high quality expressions. That's like trying to get someone to appreciate prime rib on Sunday when all they eat the rest of the week is cotton candy and bubble gum. If you have difficulty appreciating the music you hear on Sunday morning, maybe you need to make some changes to your listening habits at home.

If we want to be people who live truly godly lives and make God-pleasing decisions, we must guard our affections, for therein lies the root of our religion. If we want to be able to choose music that truly glorifies God, we must forsake those things that are shaping our affections in an unbiblical manner. This is something that greatly burdens me. How can we expect to have biblical love for God when our affections are being shaped by the movies and music of pop culture? How can we expect our teenagers to know what true, biblical love for God is when Hollywood, TV, and sports celebrities are shaping their view of love? How can we expect to have religious affections for God when our affections are being shaped by the sensual, chaotic, immoral sounds of rock music? If you want true biblical affections for the Lord that will affect your life, forsake those things! Exercise biblical discernment and rid your lives of those things that are warping your idea of what true affection is. What are you allowing to shape your affections?

For Discussion

1. What are the essential beliefs that are foundational to biblical Christianity?

2. How important to the Christian is right living?

3. Discuss how biblical affections provide the link between the head and the hands.

4. Describe the distinction between affections and passions.

5. What are some things that could ennoble the affections? Debase the passions?

CHAPTER FIVE

Pop Goes the Music:
Music, Culture, and the Church

Luther used bar tunes, didn't he? Handel's *Messiah* was pop music in his day, wasn't it? Mozart wrote for the masses, didn't he?

These questions and many others illustrate one of the strongest confusions that influence wrong musical choices in our day. People often misunderstand the nature of culture, especially how it relates to the church. Some assume that culture is simply neutral. Others confuse the concepts of folk culture, popular culture, and pop culture. Still others assume that "classical" music assumes a sort of "highbrow" mentality. A brief survey of how music, culture, and the church have interacted throughout history will serve to clear some of this confusion as we progress toward a biblical approach to music in everyday life.

Religion and culture have always been connected to some degree. A society's religious views influence the way it expresses itself in culture, and musical forms especially mirror the ties between the two. Examining how culture and church music interact can be a fascinating study.

Culture is the tangible expression of a society's collective worldview. It is religion externalized. How a particular community looks at life, morality, God, mankind, and justice expresses itself externally in their popular visual art, literature, philosophies, and music. T. S. Elliot argued, "No culture can appear or develop except in relation to a religion."[1] In other words, a society's beliefs about God affect its view of the world, and these beliefs will manifest themselves in cultural expression.

In the Old Testament period, religion and Jewish culture were intertwined so that they were inseparable. Because Israel was a theocracy, no sacred/secular distinction existed. The Israelites used the same musical and textual expressions for worship as they did for a festival, coronation, or funeral. Culture in those days was completely controlled by religion.

The Psalms readily demonstrate the close connection between religious music and culture in Jewish society. Though no music forms are evident, texts for specific religious occasions are identical in form and similar in content to those for other societal occasions. That war songs, songs for political celebrations, and even songs of personal expression are included in the religious songbook of the Jews illustrates the linked relationship between sacred music and the Israelites' culture.

This kind of connection is not true for any subsequent society to the same extent. Though relationships between religious music and culture have certainly existed, absence of an actual theocracy prohibits the same kind of relationship that Old Testament Jews experienced. The interesting question for the rest of history is, then, what kinds of relationships exist between church music and culture, and to what extent does one influence or control the other?

[1] T. S. Elliot, "Notes Towards the Definition of Culture," in *Christianity and Culture* (New York: Harcourt, Brace and World, 1949), 100.

The Early Church

The early church was essentially Jewish. "It is only natural . . . that we seek the origins of early Christian worship in Jewish temple and synagogue worship."[2] Since the church began with Jews and the earliest believers were Jews, new Christians naturally continued worshiping with Jewish traditions, adding to them new truth concerning Jesus the Messiah.

Thus, the intertwining of culture and church music continued for the early church as they had been in the Old Testament theocracy. Even as the gospel spread, Christians carried Jewish synagogue worship practices to pagan cultures. For instance, the early church continued to observe Passover (Acts 20:16, 1 Cor. 16:8),[3] and many biblical scholars consider "the prayers" in Acts 2:42 to be some form of liturgical prayers carried from synagogue practice into the early church.

It was not long, however, before the church developed a subculture of its own. As persecution increased from both pagan and Jewish fronts, Christians were forced to move underground. That would certainly have influenced worship practices, including church music, since those believers could worship only with the means at their disposal, and fear of discovery would have especially necessitated discreetness in musical expressions. Nevertheless, it is almost certain that the earliest church music was influenced heavily by Jewish culture, a culture that had been intertwined with biblical religion for centuries. How soon or to what extent that connection weakened is unclear, but the fact that the church very quickly went underground suggests that it retained the Jewish cultural forms for some time.

---

[2] Andrew E. Hill, *Enter His Courts with Praise* (Grand Rapids: Baker, 1993), 222. See also David Mappes, "The 'Elder' in the Old and New Testaments," *Bibliotheca Sacra* 154:613 (Jan-Mar 1997), 89-90.

[3] Even Paul, the great missionary to the pagans, always sought Jewish converts in a Gentile city first, and he continued to observe Jewish feasts such as Passover.

The Middle Ages

The legalization of Christianity and its subsequent establishment as the official religion of the state in the fourth century significantly influenced the relationship between the church
and culture. Essentially, a "top-heavy" church/state controlled
cultural expression with an iron fist. How could a once-illegal
church gain so much power and influence virtually overnight?
Several factors combined to create this phenomenon.

First, now that Christianity was legal and even encouraged by the Roman emperor, numerous churches sprang up
throughout the empire. In fact, so many churches were formed
during those early years that there was not enough time to train
new pastors. This prodded church leaders to publish acceptable
forms of worship for newly formed churches to follow, giving
great responsibility and power to the leaders of the church.

Second, as congregations began to grow, large buildings
were erected to accommodate the masses, and worship had
to be organized to prevent confusion. Again, powerful church
leaders formulated permissible liturgies for the churches.

Third, as heresy began to spread, proponents of such er-
rors spread their falsity through the use of hymns. That gave
church leadership cause to consolidate its power even further and demand complete control over the church's music.
Churches could use only those musical forms that were expressly sanctioned by the leadership.

Fourth, since Christianity became the official religion of
the state, virtually everyone was baptized into the church and
considered to be a believer. That gave the leadership of the
church greater power and influence since these professing believers would certainly look to them for guidance. The new
"nobles" of the empire gained significant power and wealth,

taking for themselves vast properties and creating excessive pomp and circumstance.

In addition, those church leaders looked increasingly to Old Testament traditions to formulate their theology and liturgy. That soon developed into an errant theology of priests, sacrifices, and mandatory grandeur in worship forms. Over a relatively short span of time, the simple worship practices of the early church were transformed into spectacular ceremonies full of lavish furnishings and grandiose pageantry.

All of these factors combined to form a powerful body of bishops who not only controlled church teaching and practice but also held strong influence over politics and culture. "In the millennium between 500 and 1500 the church, however errant, was . . . the strongest force in Western culture."[4]

The church's influence over culture during this period had both positive and negative effects. As the church controlled culture, it blocked explicit paganism from influencing culture, whether high culture or folk culture. The church even attempted to spread its influences over pagan cultures, as evidenced by the Crusades.

Regarding music specifically, high art was nurtured in the church itself. Almost all expressions of high art from this time period are sacred in nature. The church influenced even folk art, which takes its cues from high art but on a more popular level. A Christian perspective dominated both high and folk cultures. What the church thought and said tended to be embodied in both the official cultures (philosophy, art, concert halls, etc.) and the folk cultures (folk songs, local customs, and traditions, and so forth). A purely secular culture did not exist at that time.

---

[4] Donald Hustad, *Jubilate II: Church Music in Worship and Renewal* (Carol Stream, Ill.: Hope, 1993), 181.

Because of the glamour and spectacle of the Roman Church, church music took the form of the high art of the day. The most sophisticated musical forms found their home in church music, and performance of church music was reserved for the clergy and the musically trained. All of this was terrible news for biblical theology, but relatively good news for culture. In reality, all Western culture during the Middle Ages had at least a theistic worldview. People, at the very least, had a belief in God, although it was not often salvific. This resulted in cultural expressions, both in high art and folk art, which exhibited theistic and even biblical principles rather than secular perspectives.

The Reformation

When Martin Luther nailed his ninety-five theses to the door of the church at Wittenburg in 1517, he not only sparked a theological reformation in the church, but he also led the way for a new interaction between church music and culture. Luther had a strong conviction that every member of the congregation should have the words of Scripture on his tongue. He wanted, therefore, the music of the church to be distinctly congregational in nature. Just as he wanted the Bible to be in the German language, he also wanted the texts and the tunes of German church music to be in the vernacular.

> But I would very much like to have a true German character. For to translate the Latin text and retain the Latin tone or notes has my sanction, though it does not sound polished or well done. Both the text and notes, accent, melody, and manner of rendering ought to grow out of the

true mother tongue and its inflection; otherwise all of it becomes an imitation, in the manner of apes.[5]

Luther's knowledge of the Bible combined with his skills as a poet and musician allowed him to make great strides in the congregational music of the day. Luther's genius was combining the best sophisticated art music with accessible folk music forms. The result was the Lutheran chorale, a congregational music form that was both good and appealing.

Recognition of Luther's discernment and conservatism in his mixing church music with secular culture is important. It is clear that Luther was selective in his choices of musical idioms. Despite the plethora of more debased secular forms such as dance and drinking songs, Luther was careful to reject those with rhythms too intense for use in the church. As Robert Harrell explains, "Strongly rhythmic dance music also existed in Luther's day. The rhythms from these songs do not appear in Luther's music; rather, the rhythmic basis of the chorales lies in the word accents instead of dance rhythms."[6]

Ulrich Leupold observes, "Rollicking drinking songs were available in the 16th century too. Luther steered clear of them. He never considered music a mere tool that could be employed regardless of its original association but was careful to match text and tune, so that each text would have its own proper tune and so that both would complement each other."[7]

---

[5] Martin Luther, "Against the Heavenly Prophets in the Matter of Images and Sacraments," trans. Bernhard Erling, in *Luther's Works*, eds. Conrad Bergendoff and Helmut Lehmann, vol. 40: *Church and Ministry II*, American (Philadelphia: Muhlenberg, 1958), 141.

[6] Robert Lomas Harrell, "A Comparison of Secular Elements in the Chorales of Martin Luther with Rock Elements in Church Music of the 1960's and 1970's" (M.A. Thesis, Bob Jones University, 1975), 36.

[7] Ulrich S. Leupold, "Learning from Luther? Some Observations on Luther's Hymns," *Journal of Church Music* 8 (July-August 1966), 5.

Luther began a tradition of church music that took the best of high culture and combined it with the best of folk culture to make it accessible for average worshipers in a congregation. While the church largely influenced both high art and folk art during the Middle Ages, it was high art that comprised the majority of church music during that period. Luther encouraged congregational participation during the Reformation by eliminating from church music both the more inaccessible forms of high art and the more debased forms of folk art, thus embracing what was as excellent as it was popular. This had wonderful ramifications for church music for all those who follow in Luther's tradition.

Pietism

Often significant events in the stream of history will considerably affect culture, religion, and their interaction with one another. Such was the case with the Thirty Years' War in the mid-17th century. The horrors of that war, begun as a skirmish between Catholics and Protestants and expanding to encompass much more, left society in a state of despair and longing for comfort. Johannes Riedel describes the period, "Confronted with the horrible killing and pillaging of the Thirty Years' War, the individual sought enlightenment, self-understanding, comfort, and consolation in a personal and subjective approach to God."[8]

What resulted from these sentiments was a reaction against orthodox formalism and scholasticism and an emphasis on personal piety and experience that reached its culmination in the Pietistic movement in Germany. Pietism spread with men

---

[8] Johannes Riedel, *The Lutheran Chorale: Its Basic Traditions* (Minneapolis: Augsburg Fortress, 1967), 36.

like Jacob Spener and August Francke who maintained that the purpose of worship and church music was to build up and edify the worshiper. Such thinking had profound effects on the hymnody and other church music of the day.

The influence of Pietism produced church music that was much more personal and subjective than its predecessors. Pietistic hymn writers such as Johann Schütz, Joachim Neander, and Gerhard Tersteegen emphasized an individualistic, experiential, even sentimental aspect of Christianity. They rejected customary liturgical forms of worship in favor of simpler, personal expressions of faith. Included in this rejection was any church music that did not edify the worshiper, and church music during this period lapsed into extreme personal subjectivism. Even J. S. Bach found himself in conflict with Pietism, yet much of his church music demonstrates its influences.

The effects of Pietism were both good and bad. An emphasis on personal relationship with God was certainly helpful, but a devaluing of theology, an overemphasis on experience, and a man-centered view of congregational worship left deep voids within true Christian piety.

The Enlightenment, Rationalism, and the Industrial Revolution

Through the late 17th century, culture expressed itself along two planes, high culture and folk culture, over both of which the church had significant influence. How these two forms of culture interacted with each other and with religion changed slightly based on various influences, but nevertheless, the overall picture remained consistent. This all changed with the "Age of Reason."

Beginning in the 18ᵗʰ century, philosophers of Rationalism such as Voltaire and Rousseau slipped into the barren field left by the intellectual weaknesses of Pietism and sparked an emphasis on man's autonomy and trust in reason that permeated culture and religion alike. Religion and spirituality were now distrusted in favor of reason and science.

> In contrast to the medieval Christian cosmos, which was not only created but continuously and directly governed by a personal and actively omnipotent God, the modern universe was an impersonal phenomenon, governed by regular natural laws and understandable in exclusively physical and mathematical terms.[9]

In terms of cultural expression, progress and pleasure were now most important. The arts were expected to please rather than to instruct. People's personal tastes now shaped music. This changed culture forever. Pontynen notes, "While the traditional pursuit of beauty declines, the aesthetic pursuit of hedonistic or sanctimonious pleasure increases, and when public culture is reduced to the pursuit of pleasure, the results are not—pretty."[10]

The Enlightenment succeeded in dethroning Christian perspectives, sending the culture of the church into exile. This was the origin of a purely secular culture, which up to this time had never before existed in Western society. Now that organized religion no longer shaped culture, high culture broke off on its own and very quickly plummeted into antiquity. While high art retained good, Christianity-influenced quali-

---

[9] Tarnas, 285.
[10] Arthur Pontynen, *For the Love of Beauty* (London: Transaction, 2006), 241-242.

ties through the Classical and Romantic periods, it slowly spiraled downward in quality, interest, and production.

Folk culture, on the other hand, was soon completely replaced. Flowing from the Enlightenment and its emphasis on reason and human autonomy came the Industrial Revolution. Technological progress began to flourish. Emphasis on commercialism and the rise of mass media gave birth to a new form of culture, pop culture. Pop culture did not exist before the invention of mass media, nor did it begin to exist alongside folk culture. Pop culture destroyed folk culture. Pop culture is intrinsically commercial and secular. Whatever appeals to the masses and makes money is produced.

A common error often exists in contemporary discussions of the use of folk idioms as a compositional element in art music. Many authors today equate folk music with popular forms such as jazz, rock, and blues. In fact, the terms "folk" and "popular" have unfortunately come to be synonymous in conventional speech. For instance, George Gershwin (1898–1937) referred to his opera Porgy and Bess as an "American folk opera," although it includes distinctly pop forms such as blues and jazz.

However, an honest examination of the historical development of music will note that folk music and pop music, in the more specific sense, are in fact different in many significant ways. Certainly folk music is popular, but it is not the same as pop music in the way the term is used today to describe the commercial music of radio, film, and television. "Popular" is an adjective that simply means something that is "widely liked or appreciated."[11]

---

[11] *The American Heritage College Dictionary* (Boston: Houghton Mifflin Company, 2000), 1064.

Folk music expert Cecil Sharp recognizes the confusion between the uses of the terms "folk" and "popular" in the English language as one of semantics.

> The word itself ["folk song"] is a German compound, which of recent years has found a home in this country. Unhappily it is used in two senses. Scientific writers restrict its meaning to the song created by the unlettered classes. Others, however, use it to denote not only the peasant songs, but all popular songs as well, irrespective of origin, i.e., in the wider and looser sense in which it is sometimes used in Germany. This is to destroy the value of a very useful expression, and to rob scientists of a word of great value. The expansion was, moreover, unnecessary. For the English language already possessed in the phrase "popular song," a description which covered the wider field. There was, therefore, no need to do violence to the restricted and strictly scientific meaning of "folk song" by stretching it beyond its natural signification. On the other hand there was a very good reason for coining a new term, or for importing a foreign one, to signify a peasant-made song, because our language contained no word with that precise meaning.
>
> Those, therefore, who claim the right to use the term folk song in the loose sense of popular song, are placing upon it a meaning never given to it by the scientific writers of Germany, the country of its origin.[12]

It seems that the confusion between the terms lies primarily in the word "popular." Neither folk nor pop music is by necessity popular: it is not the defining characteristic of ei-

---

[12] Cecil Sharp, *English Folk-Song: Some Conclusions* (London: Simpkin, 1907), 2-3.

ther, yet both often are popular. Additionally, not only is the popularity of a tune not an indication of its positive value, but also, according to Sharp, it is not an indication of its negative value: "Bad tunes are popular, not because of their badness, but because of their attractiveness. The classes who sing bad tunes sing them simply because they never hear good ones that appeal to them with equal force."[13]The strength of folk music is that it is both good and popular.

Pop cultural influences quickly found their way into church music beginning with Friedrich Schleiermacher. Because church music has the primary purpose of edification, it should necessarily be accessible for every person. Church music, therefore, must be simple and expressly popular. Only church music that appealed to the "common man" would suffice for acceptable use in worship. Therefore, Schleiermacher pressed for an adoption of secular culture into church music, something that could never have been attempted before.

Such developments produced effects that greatly influenced culture and church music for years to come. The creation of secular culture, the destruction of pure folk culture and its subsequent replacement by new mass pop culture, and a fundamental distrust of religion all led to a profoundly new interaction between culture and church music that was carried well into the modern age.

American Democracy[14]

When America earned its independence and established representative democracy as the governing principle of its new

---

[13] Ibid., 174.

[14] cf. Mark A. Noll, *America's God: From Jonathan Edwards to Abraham Lincoln* (Oxford: Oxford University Press, 2002).

Constitution, free religious expression achieved great liberty. Believers of all religions now found their long sought-after freedom to worship however they pleased. Along with democracy also came the privilege of every individual to have his or her say in the workings of the government. While all of these general characteristics of democracy are certainly beneficial for religious liberty and freedom of expression, democracy's emphasis on human freedom and individuality built on the foundations of Rationalism and further helped to "popularize" religion and the music of the church. Several influences of American democracy combined to create such effects.

First, American democracy encouraged individual autonomy and fostered a distrust in organized establishment. Such thinking added to the views of Rationalism and Humanism, further influencing evangelical theology to be more anthropocentric (man-centered). Church music continued to adopt the popular styles of the secular culture in order to appeal to people. This practice was strongly encouraged by Charles G. Finney, the "Father of Revivalism." Finney was a theological Pelagian who believed conversion was not a miracle of God but an act that human means could produce. He thought that to convince people to be saved, they had to have some kind of crisis experience. To accomplish that in his revival meetings, he thought it necessary to create excitement and appeal to generate that kind of crisis. Thus Finney pressed strongly for linking the inner culture of the church with the then-new phenomenon of pop culture.

The significance of Finney's influence on culture and the church's music cannot be overestimated. Because he believed in the autonomous ability of man to change himself, he believed that revival could be produced through the wise use of means. For people to be moved in the direction of revival, they needed something fresh and new to get their attention. Novelty for its own sake was central to Finney's method. Finney would encourage people to mimic what advertisers and politicians were doing in order to affect people. As John MacArthur has described it, "[Finney] was willing to implement virtually any means that would elicit the desired response from his audiences."[15]

Charles Finney's theology and methodology of revivalism dovetailed perfectly with the humanistic philosophies of American democracy and the pop culture it was birthing. So Finney linked the success of the church to pop culture, and men like Moody, Torrey, Sunday, Graham, Sankey, Bliss, and Shea followed suit. None of them foresaw where the church's link with the then-moderate popular culture would take them.

The second influence of the principles of American democracy upon culture and church music was its insistence that all people should have equal rights. Such a principle may help secure religious freedom and equality of treatment in a depraved society, but stubborn-faced insistence on an individual's rights increased the shift toward an anthropocentric Christianity that emphasized free choice and human autonomy. These beliefs further influenced church music, both in its texts and its musical form.

In terms of text, new hymns and church anthems focused on themes such as human freedom, personal experience, and decision to change one's self more than on theocentric worship. The church experienced a radical shift from a focus on excellence in vertical worship to man-centered, evangelistic-focused purposes, and this expressed itself readily in the music

---

[15] John MacArthur, *Ashamed of the Gospel* (Wheaton: Crossway, 1993), 159.

of the church. As evangelicals continued to stress experience and appeal to man, they proceeded to embrace the music of pop culture.

The first form of pop culture that was adopted by the church was Victorianism. Victorianism was characterized by sentimentalism and art designed for the pleasure and enter-tainment of the masses. It gave people a false view of how things really were. It elevated experience and emotion above truth and reality. Christians adopted this culture, which seemed harmless enough, though they should have recognized that this sentimentalism was debasing their affections. More recognizable danger sprang up, however, with the flourishing of secular pop culture. With the invention of cinema and tele-vision, pop culture was spiraling downward, taking musical style with it.

Finally, American democracy's support of capitalism and commercialism significantly influenced culture and religion. American pop culture's chief objective is to sell. Art is no longer produced for its beauty or benefits to humanity. Pop culture emphasizes the innovative and ignores lessons of the past. It promotes instant gratification and selfishness in the consumer. And since the church has married its music with that of pop culture, church music exhibits these characteris-tics as well.

Modernism/Postmodernism

The philosophies of Rationalism and Humanism reached their culmination in expressions of the late 19th century Modernists. The philosophy of Modernism is based on ratio-nalism: All objects are to be evaluated objectively, and reason is trusted implicitly. Everything is doubted until it can be scientifically proven. Ultimately, nothing is certain since little can be proven absolutely.

Modernism emphasized the collection and observation of knowledge. It was inherently naturalistic and humanistic, denying the supernatural and championing human reason. Features of modernism such as individualism and an optimistic view of progress affected all aspects of culture, including the culture of the church.

However, scientists and philosophers soon began to question the ability to obtain objective truth and became skeptical concerning the collection of knowledge itself. What finalized the demise of Modernism was the reality of suffering and hardship through two World Wars and the increasingly escalating crime and violence around the world. Soon, reason and science were no longer trusted.

The logical successor to Modernism, then, is Postmodernism, which thrives on skepticism. Postmoderns deny the reality, if not the mere accessibility, of objective truth. They reject any authority since no absolutes exist upon which any authority may be founded. Instead of trusting reason, the Postmodern depends only on experience and intuition. This kind of thinking adversely affected culture and especially the arts because no longer was there such a thing as absolute standards of beauty. Beauty is now "in the eye of the beholder." Such lack of objectivity in musical evaluation has led to a demand for tolerance for any music style as long as an individual finds meaning for himself in that style.

Church music has adapted this sentiment to some degree by insisting that morality in music is nonexistent. An individual can determine meaning for himself with any given genre or piece of music. Proponents of contemporary Christian music styles insist that any form of music is acceptable for Christian worship:

> With certain exceptions, arts and especially music are morally relative and inherently incapable of articulating, for want of a better term, truth speech. They are essentially neutral in their ability to express belief, creed, moral and ethic exactitudes, or even world view.[16]

> "The Christian Rocker's Creed"—We hold these truths to be self-evident, that all music was created equal, that no instrument or style of music is in itself evil—that the diversity of musical expression which flows forth from man is but one evidence of the boundless creativity of our Heavenly Father.[17]

In current church music trends, all music is permissible, and anyone who insists that one musical form is more excellent or fitting for purposes of worship than another is castigated. Any amateur can write a ditty on a napkin and rise to stardom in the contemporary Christian music community. Postmodern denial of absolute standards of beauty mixed with rampant commercialism has led to a pop marketplace of substandard church music.

Conclusion

In Western history, interaction between culture and religion has been tenuous. It is very difficult to determine which influences had greater hold on the other. Clearly, however,

---

[16] Harold Best, *Music Through the Eyes of Faith* (San Francisco: Harper, 1993), 42.
[17] *Contemporary Christian Music*, November 1988, 12.

there was a fundamental shift in the 18th century with the Enlightenment. The church was dethroned as an important influence over culture, secular culture was born, and with the growing Industrial Revolution, pop culture destroyed and replaced folk culture.

With this shift, culture was no longer directed and controlled by talented musicians and church leaders. Culture was and is now controlled by mass media and commercialism. Before the shift, godly church leaders could choose from high art and folk art music that would aid their congregations best in the worship of God. Men like Martin Luther mixed good, accessible forms of high art with the best of folk art to produce a quality, yet pleasing congregational song. After Pietism, Rationalism, and the influence of men like Schleiermacher and Finney, pop culture governed church music.

In discussing the relative merits of cultures, then, we must distinguish between the three forms of culture that have existed in history: high culture, folk culture, and pop culture. Both high and folk cultures, at least prior to the Enlightenment, were controlled by a biblical worldview in Western society, and therefore developed based on positive moral qualities. Pop culture, on the other hand, developed by the will of the masses, driven by commercialism and a secular worldview void of any understanding of God.

For Discussion

1. What is culture?

2. Describe the differences between Old Testament Jewish culture and culture today.

3. Describe the differences between high culture, folk culture, and pop culture.

4. Discuss how the Enlightenment affected culture and the church.

5. Discuss the influence of Revivalism upon the interaction between the church and pop culture.

SECTION II

Music in Lifestyle Worship

CHAPTER SIX

What Does the Music Mean?

We established in chapter 1 that the Bible is the Christian's ultimate source of authority in all matters of faith and practice. However, we also noticed that the Bible does not give us all the information we need to apply its principles to daily decisions. With issues like music, therefore, we must gather pertinent information about the subject so we can apply those principles correctly.

The most foundational issue that must be addressed in discussions of music in everyday life and music in worship is the question of whether music carries meaning. Some have framed the question in terms of the morality of music, but this is perhaps misleading since only humans can be moral. Instead, we should investigate whether music carries meaning that can influence morality.

Textual Content

Given a song with lyrics, levels of meaning may be divided into four general categories. The first level of meaning is carried denotatively through its textual content. This is the most obvious form of meaning, and one that few would disregard. The song communicates propositional truth through words and phrases combined into sentences. This level of meaning is often understood as long as the listener can hear what the lyrics are saying.

Poetic Form

The second level of meaning is found in the poetic form of the text. How the words and phrases are composed governs how the text communicates to the emotions. Though the basic content of a song communicates propositional truth, meaning can never be separated from form. In other words, propositional truth is not the only truth that is communicated in songs with lyrics. The form in which that propositional truth is packaged communicates as well. For instance, take the following example of nearly synonymous words. The actual propositional truth communicated with each word is identical, or nearly so. But the connotative flavor of the second word is actually quite different from the first:

> Homeless individual: Bum
> Boy: Fellow
> Unkind individual: Jerk

The terms mean the same thing propositionally, but they have different connotations. When we evaluate poetry, we cannot stop with looking only at the propositional content. We must also look at how the lyrics express that content.

Consider two love poems. Propositionally, they both discuss love. But do they deal with the subject in the same way?

Imagine a skunk who proposes,
To his true love, surrounded by roses.
It may turn out just fine,
When she falls for his line,
But I wonder if flowers have noses?

Let me not to the marriage of true minds
   Admit impediments. Love is not love
Which alters when it alteration finds,
   Or bends with the remover to remove:
O no! It is an ever-fixed mark
   That looks on tempests and is never shaken;
It is the star to every wandering bark,
   Whose worth's unknown, although his height be taken.
Love's not Time's fool, though rosy lips and cheeks
   Within his bending sickle's compass come:
Love alters not with his brief hours and weeks,
   But bears it out even to the edge of doom.
If this be error and upon me proved,
   I never writ, nor no man ever loved.[1]

You certainly noticed that while both poems speak of love, the first is considerably more silly and the second more serious. Now the content of the first poem is silly itself, but that just proves my point. You cannot say anything serious with a limerick, or if you try, you end up looking silly yourself. I searched for an attempt at treating a serious subject in limerick form, but could not find one. I tried writing one myself but to no avail.

The point is this: some poetic forms simply cannot treat serious subjects seriously, while other forms are more capable of supporting serious subjects.

---

[1] William Shakespeare, Sonnet 116

Often even the metric composition of a poem can communicate different feelings. For instance, consider the well-known poem, "'Twas the Night Before Christmas." Look at the first couplet, and notice how the poetic form contributes to the light, humorous nature of the poem's propositional content. It might help you to read it out loud.

> 'Twas the night before Christmas and all through
> the house
> Not a creature was stirring, not even a mouse.

This poem is written in anapestic feet, that is [weak, weak, STRONG, weak, weak, STRONG]. This form gives a kind of skipping feeling that adds to the silly overall feeling of the poem's content. How does it do this? Is this simply cultural convention? In another culture, could this poetic form be interpreted as serious? Hardly. This form inherently communicates "skippiness" precisely because it *sounds* like skipping; it accurately mimics in sound what skipping feels like physically. Poets know that this accent pattern should be used for "exuberant, ecstatic texts, for a feeling of lightness comes from the use of the basic triplet movement."[2] And so it is only natural for humans to hear this "skippy" meter as light, fun, and trite.

Now what would happen if we took the same propositional content and changed the poetic form? Instead of using anapestic feet [weak, weak, STRONG], what if we changed the meter to iambic feet [weak, STRONG, weak, STRONG]? Notice how this changes the treatment of the same propositional material. Again, reading out loud may be helpful.

---

[2] Austin C. Lovelace, *The Anatomy of Hymnody* (Chicago: G. I. A. Publications, 1965), 14.

> 'Twas Christmas Eve, the house was still,
> And not a creature stirred.

Instead of feeling "skippy," this treatment feels sober and stately. Instead of expecting a fun and light event to occur later in the poem, you might expect something more serious to happen in the stillness of the night. There is a very good reason that most hymns are written in such an iambic accent pattern. Poets know this pattern is "stately and noble and is best used for those texts which are propositional."[3]

Poets can use further means to change the effect of a text in the treatment of propositional content. The use of sounds has powerful influence on the effect of a text. Certain phonemes carry effect simply because of the sounds they make (these are called phonetic intensives). They carry certain connotations because they sound like the object the word describes.[4] Here are some examples:

"fl__" – communicates movement ("flutter," "flee")
"gl__" – associated with light ("glitter," "gleam")
"sl__" or "sm__" – smoothly wet words ("slimy," "smooth")
"bl__" – word expressive of sound ("blow," "bleat")
"__tt__" – particled movement ("flutter," "glitter")
"~er" – associated with repetition ("patter," "snicker")
"~le" – associated with repetition ("trickle," "dribble")
"~ck" – sudden cessation of movement ("click," "flick")

Furthermore, how words are put together into sentences can influence the text's effect based on combinations of

---

[3] Ibid., 13.
[4] It is also interesting to note that many of these phonemes are present in words that describe the same object from other languages.

sound. A perfect example is a couplet by Robert Frost. Notice how different the two lines sound from each other and how that difference reflects the propositional content of those lines. Again, read it aloud.

> The old dog barks backward without getting up.
> I can remember when he was a pup.

The use of strong plosives (b's, k's, d's, etc.) take longer to articulate, communicating the lethargy of the old dog. One could not read the line quickly if he tried. However, the phonemes in the second line easily roll off the tongue, communicating the sprightliness of the puppy.

The point of all this is that the propositional truth content of a text should not be the only criterion in an evaluation of a text's meaning. The poetic form contributes heavily to the text's ability to communicate to man's affections. Otherwise, why set the words to poetry at all? It is true that poetry aids in the retention of truth, but is this its only function? Certainly not. The primary purpose of all art is to speak to the affections.

This is important because when we evaluate what music means and whether its meaning is compatible with biblical Christianity, we must not evaluate only the propositional content of the text, but we must also evaluate the form to determine if the emotional content is appropriate.

Associative Meaning

The third level of meaning is purely associative. For instance, listening to an orchestral version of our national anthem may engender pride and patriotism for some but certainly not for all. Someone may hear "Amazing Grace," and because he has some specific experiential connection with the hymn, it will "mean" something very specific to him that it does not to the person next to him.

This level of meaning will matter in our evaluation of music only if one of two things is true. First, if the association is a shadow of intrinsic meaning (discussed below). Though associations do not make music mean something particular, they are sometimes clear indicators of what the music is really saying. For instance, just because a style of music is associated with a bar does not make it wrong for a Christian. But the fact that it is used often in taverns may be a good indication that the music is intrinsically communicating messages that fit with the tavern lifestyle. Likewise, the tune to the national anthem does intrinsically express majesty, which connects easily with pride and patriotism. Examining associations sometimes helps us to determine intrinsic meaning.

The only other reason that association might affect our evaluation of music is if it carries a negative cultural meaning now. In other words, if a certain song or style of music communicates something negative in our current culture—even if that meaning is not intrinsic—it is significant for the Christian.

Intrinsic Meaning

The deepest level of meaning is intrinsic. By intrinsic we mean that the very nature of the music carries meaning. The meaning is not because of a text, associations, or culture. The form of the music itself holds meaning. This meaning exists for the same reason we say that certain willow trees "weep" or pug dogs look "sad." They each resemble emotional characteristics common to mankind. The long droopiness of a weeping willow resembles the physical characteristics of someone who is downtrodden or depressed. The natural curvature of a pug's mouth resembles a frown. Neither the tree or pug actually possesses emotion, but we describe them in terms of emotion because they resemble the physical characteristics of certain emotions. In a very similar manner, music can carry emotional meaning by resembling the physical characteristics inherently connected with emotion through sound. John Hospers explains the connection between music and human emotion by arguing that music can mimic natural physical expressions of emotion.

> For there are times when we can say that, quite objectively, this expresses that. We can do it with regard to human facial expressions and gestures; this one expresses grief, another expresses perturbation, another jubilation, and so on. We know that this facial configuration expresses grief because when we feel grief we behave so-and-so and have such-and-such facial features. When we feel joy or disturbance we have other facial features. And this is quite objective: everyone recognizes in general what facial features are expressive of what inner states. Tears go with sadness and smiles with gladness, and this is just an objective fact. Anyone who said that furrowed brows and menacing gestures were expressive of joy or relaxation would be wrong. Now, if publicly observable facial features and gestures can be expressive, why cannot publicly observable patterns of sounds or colors also be so?[5]

Humans express primary emotions such as happiness, sadness, fear, and anger with the same outward, observable

---

[5]   John Hospers. "Aesthetics, Problems of," *Introductory Readings in Aesthetics*. (New York: The Macmillan Company & The Free Press, 1967), 164.

manifestations. For instance, humans in any culture at any time are generally slow and downtrodden when they are sad, jittery and tense when they are afraid, and fast and intense when they are angry. In a sense, this is one unified "culture of humanity" of which all people are part. These universals begin to break down when we consider more specific higher emotions such as hope, anxiety, jealousy, or shame, but primary emotions are manifested in the same ways universally. Therefore, when music aurally reflects outward physical manifestations of human emotion, it can be said to express those emotions. Bouwsma gives examples of this phenomenon, "Sad music has some of the characteristics of people who are sad. It will be slow, not tripping; it will be low, not tinkling. People who are sad move more slowly, and when they speak, they speak softly and low."[6]

Music that aurally reproduces these universal outward manifestations will universally communicate the primary emotions to which those manifestations are attached. In other words, if a certain piece of music is loud, fast, and intense, it is probably mimicking anger. Now to speak this simplistically is somewhat suspicious. Obviously we cannot narrow a musical composition down to just three moods — music is far more complex. But music uses combinations of melody, tempo, dynamics, rhythm, etc. to reproduce natural human emotional responses. In doing so, it carries intrinsic meaning. And in reality, deep musical examination is not required to discern this meaning. Any observant person knows when music communicates the exact opposite of what someone insists that does.

---

[6] O.K. Bouwsma, "The Expression Theory of Art," in *Aesthetics and Language*, ed. W. Elton (Oxford: Oxford University Press, 1952), 99.

"No lullaby will work if yelled jerkily at a brisk rate and no war march will have the desired effect if crooned mellifluously at a snail's pace."[7]

". . . loud, fast music is arousing, whilst soft, slow music is soothing."[8]

"If someone were to insist that a fast sprightly waltz was really sad or melancholy, we would refer him to the behavioral features of sad people and show him that when people are in that state they do exhibit the qualities in question (i.e., the qualities of sad music), rather than speed or sprightliness."[9]

Even the Bible relates music's power to its ability to express emotion. William Edgar notes, "Of the more than six hundred references to music in the Scriptures, the great majority connect it with some kind of emotional experience."[10] He further points out that in some cases "the instruments themselves are able to convey joy (see Ps. 45:8; 71:22; 92:1-4)," and "sometimes in the Bible the instruments themselves are personified in terms of emotional values. A lyre may be sweet (Ps. 81:2); the harp and lyre may be roused from slumber (Ps. 57:8; 108:2)."[11]

Common human experience also attests to the truth of intrinsic meaning in music. The typical department store or restaurant recognizes this fact. Major studies have been conducted to determine what styles of music encourage shopping

[7] Philip Tagg, *Fernando the Flute.* (Goteborg, Sweden: Gothenberg University, 1981), 186-187.
[8] John Sloboda, The Musical Mind: The Cognitive Psychology of Music. (Oxford: Clarendon), 1985, 1.
[9] Hospers, 47.
[10] William Edgar, *Taking Note of Music* (London: SPCK Publishing, 1986), 65.
[11] Ibid., 65-66.

or eating. Classical music is compiled into CDs called, "Power Classics" and "The Ultimate Relaxation CD" because those songs communicate what the title indicates. Clearly, music communicates certain moods that are transmitted through human emotion. A good example of this is when David used music to affect Saul's emotions (1 Sam. 16:23).

Difficulty arises when we try to nail down exactly what the meaning is. Music does not carry meaning in terms of propositions. However, when we try to evaluate exactly what music is communicating, we must do so in terms of propositional statements: "That music means X." This is inherently inaccurate because any time we try to summarize the abstract in terms of propositions, we are bound to overstate. It is like trying to summarize how you feel. It cannot always be done with complete accuracy. This provides a difficulty when evaluating music, but it does not imply that we should not still strive to come to conclusions regarding what kinds of meaning are appropriate for believers.

Toward a Taxonomy of Musical Elements

It would be unwise and unhelpful to attempt to compile a fully comprehensive list of what various musical elements express. It would be unwise because a piece of music must be evaluated as a whole — claiming that a certain beat pattern is sinful is often much too simplistic. However, because of the close connection between music's movements of sound and the movements of human expressions of emotion, musical experts do agree on a limited taxonomy of the expressive nature of musical elements. Gordon C. Bruner II demonstrates this point in a very interesting article called "Music, Mood, and Marketing" in the *Journal of Marketing*.[12] In a discussion of how marketing researchers study music and its power to effect mood, Bruner provides a helpful table demonstrating emotional expressions connected to various components of music. This is a good starting point for a simple taxonomy of expressive musical elements. Again, this kind of list will not help us pinpoint the moral effects of music perfectly, but it at least helps us to understand how music communicates.

I offer this list simply as an example of how music can express emotion by mimicking human emotional behaviors. As you read through the list, notice the connections between how humans act and feel when they experience certain emotions, and the kinds of movements and sounds the music produces. Bruner places elements into three categories: time-related expressions, pitch-related expressions, and texture-related expressions.

Time-Related Expressions

1. Duple rhythms produce a rigid and controlled expression in comparison with triple rhythm, which is more relaxed or abandoned.

2. The faster the tempo, the more animation and happiness are expressed.

3. Even, rhythmic movement can represent the unimpeded flow of some feeling; dotted, jerky, uneven rhythms produce more complex expressions.

4. Firm rhythms suggest a serious mood whereas smooth-flowing rhythms are more playful.

---

[12] *Journal of Marketing* Vol. 54, No. 4 (Oct. 1990), 94-104, by Gordon C. Bruner II. Copyright 1990 by American Marketing Association. Reproduced with permission.

5. Staccato notes give more emphasis to a passage than legato notes.

Pitch-Related Expressions

1. "Up" and "down" in pitch not only correspond to up and down in the physical world, but can also imply "out-and-in" as well as "away-and-back," respectively.

2. Rising and falling pitch can convey a growing or diminishing intensity in a given emotional context.

3. Songs in higher keys are generally considered to be happier than songs in lower keys.

4. Music in the major mode expresses more animated and positive feelings than music in the minor mode.

5. Complex harmonies are more agitated and sad than simple harmonies, which are more serene and happy.

Texture-Related Expressions

1. Loudness can suggest animation or proximity whereas low volume implies tranquility or distance.

2. Crescendo (soft to loud) expresses an increase in force whereas diminuendo (loud to soft) suggests a decrease in power.

3. The timbre of brass instruments conveys a feeling of cold, hard force whereas reed instruments produce a lonely, melancholy expression.

Bruner then provides an impressive list of research that supports such conclusions. Another very interesting table provided by Bruner is a list of how combinations of various musical elements can very strongly express certain emotions:

Serious Emotional Expression
    Mode: Major
    Tempo: Slow
    Pitch: Low
    Rhythm: Firm
    Harmony: Consonant
    Volume: Medium

Sad Emotional Expression
    Mode: Minor
    Tempo: Slow
    Pitch: Low
    Rhythm: Firm
    Harmony: Dissonant
    Volume: Soft

Sentimental Emotional Expression
    Mode: Minor
    Tempo: Slow
    Pitch: Medium
    Rhythm: Flowing
    Harmony: Consonant
    Volume: Soft

Serene Emotional Expression
    Mode: Major
    Tempo: Slow

Pitch: Medium
Rhythm: Flowing
Harmony: Consonant
Volume: Soft

Humorous Emotional Expression
    Mode: Major
    Tempo: Fast
    Pitch: High
    Rhythm: Flowing
    Harmony: Consonant
    Volume: Medium

Happy Emotional Expression
    Mode: Major
    Tempo: Fast
    Pitch: High
    Rhythm: Flowing
    Harmony: Consonant
    Volume: Medium

Exciting Emotional Expression
    Mode: Major
    Tempo: Fast
    Pitch: Medium
    Rhythm: Uneven
    Harmony: Dissonant
    Volume: Loud

Majestic Emotional Expression
    Mode: Major
    Tempo: Medium

Pitch: Medium
Rhythm: Firm
Harmony: Dissonant
Volume: Loud

Frightening Emotional Expression
Mode: Minor
Tempo: Slow
Pitch: Low
Rhythm: Uneven
Harmony: Dissonant
Volume: Varied

Such lists are not essential for someone wanting to determine what music means. Since all humans share emotional responses, interpreting music's relation to those responses is fairly simple. However, these kinds of lists are helpful for those who are interested in studying meaning in music more carefully.

Conclusion

Music carries meaning, and Christians must evaluate that meaning to determine whether it is appropriate for them. If believers are concerned to pursue holiness, and if they are willing to take important biblical principles and apply them to every area of their lives (including the music they enjoy), they must be willing to evaluate meaning in music to determine whether that meaning fits with God's desires.

For Discussion

1. Explain how poetry carries meaning beyond simply the propositional content.

2. Discuss the importance of association in determining meaning in music.

3. Discuss how music can intrinsically carry emotional meaning.

CHAPTER SEVEN

Beauty and Glory

We have discussed at length the moral influence of the texts and tunes of music, but what about the deeper aesthetic qualities of music? What about beauty? Is beauty discussed at all in the Bible? This chapter will show that beauty is more than "in the eye of the beholder." Beauty is directly linked to the glory of God.

Defining Glory

Most Christians would acknowledge that their primary objective is to glorify God, but what exactly does that mean? The glory of God is often a nebulous concept that warrants explanation for one seeking to please God with his musical choices.

Jonathan Edwards' thorough treatment of God's principal aim inevitably led him to attempt to define God's glory. Edwards essentially argues that the glory of something is what "signifies excellency, dignity, or worthiness of regard." He cites multiple Scripture passages to illustrate that "the word glory is very commonly used to signify the excellency of a person or thing, as consisting either in greatness, or in beauty, or in both conjunctly."[1] For Edwards, "glory" is the express manifestation of this inner beauty. He notes that Scripture often speaks of glory in terms of "shining brightness, by an emanation of beams of light." He compares this "brightness" to that of the sun or moon, their glory being the brilliant emanation of their inner beauty.[2] In other words, according to Edwards, God's glory is essentially His beauty. In commenting on God's glory being His highest end, contemporary theologian John Piper summarizes well the connection between glory and beauty:

> Glory is not easy to define. It is like beauty. How would you define beauty? Some things we have to point at rather than define. But let me try. God's glory is the beauty of His manifold perfections. It can refer to the bright and awesome radiance that sometimes breaks forth in visible manifestations. Or it can refer to the infinite moral excellence of His character. In either case it signifies a reality of infinite greatness and worth.[3]

Other theologians define God's glory as essentially His beauty and emphasize it in terms of admirability. For instance, C. S. Lewis explains the proper response to the glory of God: "But the ascription of glory to God should be seen as a response to the glory that is inherent in his being. Before our recognition and praise, God is in himself all glory in a sublime conjunction of beauty, truth and love. This glory is majestic. It brings wonder and awe and worship."[4]

---

[1] Jonathan Edwards, "The End For Which God Created the World," in John Piper, *God's Passion for His Glory: Living the Vision of Jonathan Edwards* (Wheaton: Crossway Books, 1998), 231.
[2] Ibid., 233.
[3] John Piper, 43.
[4] C. S. Lewis, *The Weight of Glory and Other Addresses* (Grand Rapids: Eerdmans, 1965), 54.

The terms used to describe God's glory in Scripture further confirm its connection with beauty. Richard Viladesau notes, "The theologically significant content of the idea of 'beauty' is found in the Scriptures, primarily under the category of 'glory'."[5] Patrick Sherry lists various Old Testament Hebrew aesthetic terms that are used to describe God: *no am*, often translated "beauty" or "sweetness"; *hah-dahr*, rendered "splendor" or "majesty"; *tiphahrah*, translated "splendor," "pride," "glory," and "beauty", and *yophee*, translated "beauty" and probably the most aesthetically-charged Hebrew word used to describe God.[6] Edwards focuses on the term "glory" itself, most often a translation of the Hebrew word *kabod*. He observes that its root form, *kabad*, usually "signifies to be heavy" or "weighty." The noun form, *kabod*, "signifies gravity, heaviness, greatness, and abundance." He cites numerous Scripture passages to demonstrate this term's use to describe density or magnitude.[7]

Indeed, Scripture's ascription of aesthetic beauty to God is not sparse. Consider the following examples of the Scripture's descriptions of the beauty of God, using aesthetically charged words like beauty, excellence, glory, honor, majesty, and splendor:

> And when he had consulted with the people, he appointed those who should sing to the LORD, and who should praise the beauty of holiness (2 Chron. 20:21).

> Have you an arm like God? Or can you thunder with a voice like His? Then adorn yourself with majesty and splendor, And array yourself with glory and beauty (Job 40:9-10).

---

[5] Richard Viladesau, *Theological Aesthetics: God in Imagination, Beauty, and Art* (New York: Oxford University Press, 1999), 105.

[6] Patrick Sherry, *Spirit and Beauty* (London: SCM Press, 2002), 56-57.

[7] Edwards, "End," 230.

O LORD, our Lord, How excellent is Your name in all the earth! (Ps. 8:9).

One thing I have desired of the LORD, That will I seek: That I may dwell in the house of the LORD All the days of my life, To behold the beauty of the LORD, And to inquire in His temple (Ps. 27:4).

You are fairer than the sons of men; Grace is poured upon Your lips; Therefore God has blessed You forever. Gird Your sword upon Your thigh, O Mighty One, With Your glory and Your majesty. And in Your majesty ride prosperously because of truth, humility, and righteousness; And Your right hand shall teach You awesome things (Ps. 45:2-4).

Bless the LORD, O my soul! O LORD my God, You are very great: You are clothed with honor and majesty (Ps. 104:1).

All Your works shall praise You, O LORD, And Your saints shall bless You. They shall speak of the glory of Your kingdom, And talk of Your power, To make known to the sons of men His mighty acts, And the glorious majesty of His kingdom (Ps. 145:10-12).

They shall lift up their voice, they shall sing; For the majesty of the LORD They shall cry aloud from the sea (Isa. 24:14).

Let grace be shown to the wicked, Yet he will not learn righteousness; In the land of uprightness he will deal unjustly, And will not behold the majesty of the LORD (Isa. 26:10).

It shall blossom abundantly and rejoice, Even with joy and singing. The glory of Lebanon shall be given to it, The excellence of Carmel and Sharon. They shall see the glory of the LORD, The excellency of our God (Isa. 35:2).

For how great is his goodness, and how great his beauty! (Zech. 9:17 ESV).

The Bible is replete with such aesthetic references to God.

We should not go any further here without defining beauty. The traditional definition comes from a theologian, Thomas Aquinas. In his *Summa Theologica*, Aquinas reasons, "the beautiful is something pleasant to apprehend."[8] Beauty is what brings pleasure to the observer. Yet something is not beautiful *because* it brings pleasure; it brings pleasure *because* it is beautiful. Beauty resides in the properties of an object, not in the subjective opinions of the observer. As Mortimer Adler observes, "We call the object beautiful because it has certain properties that make it admirable. It has those properties whether or not its having them results in its being enjoyable by you or me."[9]

An assertion that a flower or a sunset or a work of art is "beautiful" is, by implication, an acknowledgment of the absolute nature of beauty. The absolute nature of beauty is especially evident in what people consider ugly. No one would delight in a cesspool or landfill. Yet this assumption of objectivity in aesthetics has proven problematic throughout history. If an object indeed has certain properties whereby it can be determined to be beautiful, from whence comes its objectivity? Most

---

8   Thomas Aquinas, *Aquinas's Shorter Summa: Saint Thomas's Own Concise Version of His Summa Theologica* (Manchester, N.H.: Sophia Institute Press, 2001), 320.
9   Mortimer Adler, *Six Great Ideas* (New York: Collier Books, 1981), 112.

have tried to answer the question by connecting the properties of beauty with universal principles, that is, principles rooted in creation. For example, Pythagoras (6th century B.C.), arguably the earliest aesthetician, discovered numerical relationships governing the basic intervals of music and attributed the craft and beauty of music to its underpinning universal principles.[10] Pythagorean thought established absolute standards for aesthetics and had significant influence over later philosophers, including Plato, Augustine, and Boethius, and theologians, including Luther, Calvin, and Edwards. According to these philosophers and theologians, music that corresponds to these universals will, by these standards, be beautiful and will give pleasure to the observer.

This connection between beauty and pleasure is important for our discussion because C. S. Lewis also makes a similar connection between praise of God's glory and pleasure. Lewis admits that the concept of praise in Scripture often confounded him until he compared it to common praise on a daily basis. He describes this comparison so vividly that it warrants complete quotation:

> But the most obvious fact about praise — whether of God or any thing — strangely escaped me. I thought of it in terms of compliment, approval, or the giving of honor. I had never noticed that all enjoyment spontaneously overflows into praise unless (sometimes even if) shyness or the fear of boring others is deliberately brought in to check it. The world rings with praise — lovers praising their mistresses, readers their favorite poet, walkers praising the countryside, players praising their favorite game — praise of weather, wines,

10 Piero Weiss and Richard Taruskin, *Music in the Western World: A History in Documents* (Belmont, Calif.: Schirmer, 1984), 3-7.

dishes, actors, motors, horses, colleges, countries, historical personages, children, flowers, mountains, rare stamps,
rare beetles, even sometimes politicians or scholars. I had
not noticed how the humblest, and at the same time most
balanced and capricious, minds, praised most, while the
cranks, misfits and malcontents praised least . . .

I had not noticed either that just as men spontaneously
praise whatever they value, so they spontaneously urge us
to join them in praising it: "Isn't she lovely? Wasn't it glorious? Don't you think that magnificent?" The Psalmists in
telling everyone to praise God are doing what all men do
when they speak of what they care about. My whole, more
general difficulty about the praise of God depended on my
absurdly denying to us, as regards the supremely Valuable,
what we delight to do, what indeed we can't help doing,
about everything else we value.

I think we delight to praise what we enjoy because the
praise not merely expresses but completes the enjoyment;
it is its appointed consummation. It is not out of compli-
ment that lovers keep on telling one another how beautiful they are; the delight is incomplete till it is expressed.[11]

Thus praise is not simply a duty; it is a delight—pleasure
in the splendor of God. That is why Piper changes the answer
to the first question of the Westminster Catechism from "The
chief end of man is to glorify God and enjoy him forever" to
"The chief end of man is to glorify God BY enjoying him forever."[12] God's people glorifying Him is essentially delighting

[11] C. S. Lewis, *Reflections on the Psalms* (New York: Harcourt, Brace and World, 1958), 126.
[12] Piper, *Desiring God*, 15.

in Him because of His unique qualities. This kind of delight is tantamount to aesthetic pleasure. Thus glorifying God is taking aesthetic pleasure in His unique excellences.

A further important consideration regarding God's glory as His "beauty" is the manner in which it is apprehended. Edwards argues that delight in the beauty of God is a "view or knowledge of God's excellency."[13] This observation has two implications: (1) that the beauty of God, as with all beauty, resides in His objective qualities; and (2) that the pleasure resulting from apprehension of such beauty is not merely physical but intellectual. Edwards expands upon the second of these implications in *The Religious Affections*. When Edwards describes the pleasure, or "affections," that result from an apprehension of God's beauty, he is not describing a merely physical faculty separate from the understanding or will. He is describing the "inclination of the will," that is, that which moves the soul to appreciate the object.[14] So, for Edwards, pleasure taken in the knowledge of the beauty of God is not merely physical, it is a delight of the mind. This is all significant for a discussion of music since the definitions of both aesthetic beauty and the glory of God are essentially the same, implying an inevitable link between the two for the Christian.

Thus God can rightly be described as beautiful, for Scripture's aesthetic terminology and the very concept of His glory are indeed His beauty. This is so much the case that Augustine could actually refer to God as "beauty."

Too late I loved You, Beauty of Ancient Days, yet ever new!
Too late I loved You! Behold, You were within me, and I

---

[13]   Edwards, "End," 237.
[14]   Jonathan Edwards, *The Religious Affections* (Carlisle, Pa.: The Banner of Truth Trust, 2001), 96-97.

was outside of You. There I searched for You, I who was deformed, plunging amid those beautiful things which You had made. You were with me, but I was not with You. Things held me far from You, which, unless they were in You, would not exist at all. You called and shouted and burst my deafness. You flashed, shone, and shattered my blindness. You breathed aromas, and I drew in breath, and now I pant for You. I tasted You, and now I hunger and thirst. You touched me, and I burned for Your peace.[15]

The Source of Beauty

Augustine's ascription of beauty to God relates to Edwards' observation that delight in the beauty of God is a "view or knowledge of God's excellency"—that God is indeed the absolute source of all beauty. He is absolute beauty. Belief that God is beauty implies that all earthly forms of beauty flow from Him as well. As Clyde S. Kilby notes, "To believe in God involves accepting him as the sovereign perfection, not only of truth and goodness but also of beauty, thus establishing the highest possible conceptions of excellence."[16] Aquinas himself argued that since God is the greatest beauty, He is therefore the source of all beauty.[17]

If God is supreme beauty and, therefore, the source of all earthly beauty, it follows that earthly beauty, including beauty in music, is a reflection of the divine. Surely God's own creation must have been beautiful since it was formed by the hand of Beauty Himself. In the Genesis account of

---

[15] Augustine, *The Confessions of Saint Augustine* (New Kensington, Pa.: Whitaker House, 1996), 276.

[16] Kilby, *Christianity and Aesthetics* (Chicago: InterVarsity Press, 1961), 22.

[17] Viladesau, 116.

creation, God affirmed that His creation was indeed beautiful by calling it "good."[18] Spiegel notes that this judgment of the "goodness" (*tov* in the Hebrew) of His creation could not have referred to its moral excellence since "moral evaluations properly apply only to persons or their actions."[19] Furthermore, Kilby notes, "since we say such things only of acts we have pleasure in, the Great Artist was evidently much pleased with his world."[20] Therefore, "good" must refer to aesthetic excellence, and indeed *tov* as well as its Greek equivalent *kala* often designate beauty.[21]

Nature may be called "beautiful" inasmuch as it reflects the absolute standard of God's beauty. Hans Urs von Balthasar states that "the cosmos is experienced as the representation and manifestation of the hidden transcendent beauty of God,"[22] and both Edwards and Kuyper attribute that representation to observable qualities such as "regularity, order, uniformity, symmetry, proportion, harmony, etc." and "balance, rhythm, symmetry, proportion, etc."[23] Indeed, as Edwards wrote, "The beauty of the world is a communication

---

[18] Genesis 1:4, 10, 12, 18, 21, and 25.

[19] James S. Spiegel, "Aesthetics and Worship." *Southern Baptist Journal of Theology* (Winter, 1998): 41-42.

[20] Kilby, 18.

[21] *Kala* is the term that the translators who produced the Greek translation of the Old Testament used to translate *tov*. This same word was used in Homer's *The Odyssey* when Odysseus describes the dog Argos as "handsome in body" (New York: W. W. Norton, 1967), 236. See Brown, *Good Taste* (Oxford: University Press, 2000), 100.

[22] Hans Urs von Balthasar, *The Glory of the Lord: A Theological Aesthetics*, ii. trans. Andrew Louth et al. (San Francisco: Ignatius Press, 1984), 154.

[23] Jonathan Edwards, *The Nature of True Virtue* (Ann Arbor: The University of Michigan Press, 1960), 27-28; Kuyper, *Het Calvinisme en de Kunst*, 17; quoted in Begbie, *Voicing Creation's Praise* (London: Continuum, 1991), 97.

of God's beauty."[24] Thus, these properties in nature and art create beauty expressly because they are the same properties that comprise the beauty of God.

The Bible itself—a product of God's hand—is an example of artistic beauty. Kilby observes, "The Bible comes to us in an artistic form which is often sublime [beautiful], rather than as a document of practical, expository prose, strict in outline like a textbook."[25] He asserts that this beauty is not merely decorative but part of the essential presentation of its truth: "We do not have truth and beauty, or truth decorated with beauty, or truth illustrated by the beautiful phrase, or truth in a 'beautiful setting.' Truth and beauty are in the Scriptures, as indeed they must always be, an inseparable unity."[26] Furthermore, since the Bible is a production of men moved by the Holy Spirit of God, it is a prime example of the aesthetically creative work of both God and men.[27]

This leads to an observation of man-made art in Scripture upon which God passes aesthetic judgment. For instance, God gives explicit artistic guidelines for His temple and liturgical adornments, which He says were specifically designed for "glory and beauty." Such meticulous guidelines are listed in Exodus 25-28, 36-39, 1 Kings 6-7, and 2 Chronicles 2-3. Man, as God's image-bearer, can actually create beautiful objects by imitating the beautiful properties of God in his craft.

Balthasar is right when he says, "God's beauty is his most neglected attribute."[28] Yet Scriptural descriptions of God

---

[24] Jonathan Edwards, *The Miscellanies* (Entry Nos. a-z, aa–zz, 1-500), ed. Thomas A. Schafer (New Haven: Yale University Press, 1994), 384.

[25] Kilby, 19.

[26] Ibid., 21.

[27] Ibid.

[28] Hans Urs von Balthasar, *Word and Revelation* (New York: Herder and Herder, 1964), 162.

include distinctly aesthetic terminology. God is transcendental beauty and is, therefore, the ultimate source of all earthly beauty. Thus anything that reflects His absolute perfections can rightly be called "beautiful."

Music — Pointing to God

Because earthly beauty is a reflection of God's beauty—His glory—then earthly beauty can actually reveal to men something of the nature of God. The idea that beauty points to God is not novel. Viladesau notes that this notion was, in fact, "one of the fundamental and leading motifs of medieval theology."[29] He asserts, "The medieval West saw an 'objective' connection of music and the arts with the sacred because they are concerned with re-creating or representing the beautiful order given to the world by the Creator."[30] Theologians have long agreed that God's beauty is manifest in both creation and man-made art. Psalm 19:1 reveals nature's role in displaying God's beauty when it says, "The heavens declare the glory of God," and inasmuch as art reflects creation, it can also manifest God's glory. Additionally, Romans 1:20 records that "For his invisible attributes, namely, his eternal power and divine nature, have been clearly perceived, ever since the creation of the world, in the things that have been made" (ESV). Thus, like beauty in God's creation, beauty in music is a form of general, non-salvific revelation.[31]

---

[29] Viladesau, 108.

[30] Ibid., 151.

[31] Theologians speak of two forms of revelation: "general revelation," that which attests to "God's existence, character, and moral law, which comes through creation to all humanity"; and "special revelation," that which "refers to God's words addressed to specific people." Only through the special revelation of the Bible can one come to a saving knowledge of God. See Wayne Grudem, *Systematic Theology,* 122-123.

Successfully reflecting God's divine glory in music glorifies
Him because in reflecting God's glory, His beauty is magnified.
In other words, by taking delight in certain objects because of
their beautiful properties, we are implying they are indeed worthy of delight. And since those properties are worthy, particularly because they are part of God's essence, we are affirming
that He is ultimately worthy of our delight. This is true not
only of explicitly sacred music; even truly beautiful secular music when compared to God brings Him glory. Conversely, if we
call something beautiful that does not possess the properties of
God's beauty, we fail to bring God the glory due Him.

Yearning for Supreme Beauty

Earthly beauty does more than just reveal God's creative
hand, however. The finite pleasures produced through earthly
beauty produce a yearning for more satisfying pleasure in infinite beauty. C. S. Lewis argues that before man's fall into sin
and subsequent corruption, he had gratifying pleasure that is
now left wanting.

> There once was in man a true happiness of which now
> remain to him only the mark and empty trace, which he
> in vain tries to fill from all his surroundings, seeking from
> things absent the help he does not obtain in things pres-
> ent. But these are all inadequate, because the infinite abyss
> can only be filled by an infinite and immutable object,
> that is to say, only by God Himself.[32]

In other words, every man seeks pleasure in things like
music, but music can fulfill that longing only in a limited

---

[32] Lewis, *The Weight of Glory*, 113.

sense. Blaise Pascal argues that this desire for happiness is innate within every man:

> All men seek happiness. This is without exception. Whatever different means they employ, they all tend to this end. The cause of some going to war, and of others avoiding it, is the same desire in both, attended with different views. The will never takes the least step but to this object. This is the motive of every action of every man, even of those who hang themselves.[33]

Since apprehension of beauty produces a measure of pleasure, the observer gains a profound, yet fleeting taste of what he is ultimately seeking. In this sense, "beauty has the strange effect of at once beckoning us to itself and pointing beyond itself to that which seems tantalizingly unattainable. It draws us to itself and through itself."[34] Thus every apprehension of beauty further increases a deep yearning for something more, a pleasure that will not fade away. As Kilby notes, "How perfectly the writer of Ecclesiastes put it when he said, 'The eye is not satisfied with seeing, nor the ear filled with hearing'" (Eccl. 1:8 ESV).[35]

This longing for infinite pleasure, and thus infinite beauty, is something that is fixed into the soul of every man. Kuyper insists, "Our being cannot be satisfied unless the thirst for beauty is quenched. That is why the child of God fights for beauty and holiness, because at the creation man was absolutely beautiful."[36] In this way man cannot suppress his innate

---

[33] Blaise Pascal, *Pascal's Pensées*, trans. by W. F. Trotter (New York: E. P. Dutton, 1958), 113.

[34] Harries, *Art and the Beauty of God: A Christian Understanding* (New York: Continuum, 1993), 42.

[35] Kilby, 16.

[36] Abraham Kuyper, *De Gemeene Gratie*, 4, Vol. 3 (Kampen: Kok, nd), 546-547; quoted in Begbie, 97.

knowledge of God. He may suppress truth, but he cannot suppress the longing for real joy. Experiences of pleasure in earthly beauty are always temporary, and as Gregory of Nyssa once commented,

> Hope always draws the soul from the beauty which it seeks to what is beyond, always kindles the desire for the hidden through what is constantly perceived. Therefore the ardent lover of beauty, although receiving what is always visible as an image of what he desires, yet longs to be filled with the very stamp of the archetype. And the bold request which goes up the mountains of desire asks this: to enjoy the Beauty not in mirrors and reflections, but face to face."[37]

This feeling of yearning for more pleasure is one that few would deny. But for the Christian, this longing does not have to be frustrating. Not only can he take pleasure in the beauty of God in this life, but as Lewis explains, he can also look forward to an eternity reveling in the pleasure of divine beauty:

> We do not want merely to see beauty... We want something else that can hardly be put into words—to be united with the beauty we see, to pass into it, to receive it into ourselves, to bathe in it, to become part of it. That is why we have peopled air and earth and water with gods and goddesses and nymphs and elves—that, though we cannot, yet these projections can enjoy themselves that beauty, grace and power of which nature is the image... For if we take the imagery of Scripture seriously, if we believe that God will one day give us the morning star and calls us to put on the ancient myth

---

[37] Gregory of Nyssa, *The Life of Moses*, ii, 231-2 (PG 401d-404a), trans. Malherbe and Ferguson (New York: Paulist Press, 1978), 114f., quoted in Patrick Sherry, *Spirit and Beauty* (London: SCM Press, 2002), 62-63.

and the modern poetry, so false as history, we may be very near the truth as prophecy. At present we are on the outside of the world, the wrong side of the door. We discern the freshness and purity of morning, but they do not make us fresh and pure. We cannot mingle with the splendours we see. But all the leaves of the New Testament are rustling with the rumour that it will not always be so. Some day, God willing, we shall get in. When human souls have become perfect in voluntary obedience as the inanimate creation is in its lifeless obedience, then they will put on its glory, or rather that greater glory which nature is only the first sketch... We are summoned to pass in through nature, beyond her, into that splendour which she fitfully reflects.[38]

This is what all aestheticians seek in their expedition for the source of absolute beauty. As Kuyper points out, "The beautiful and the good for which Plato was searching will come when the Lord returns."[39] Thus one of the most significant functions of beautiful music is to give the listener a finite taste of the joy that one can have in God. As Psalm 16:11 states, "In your presence is fullness of joy; At Your right hand are pleasures forevermore." Music must give the listener pleasure in such a way that he will then yearn for and seek after God.

The Danger of Beauty

I have shown how music can point to God in the thinking of many theologians, but that is not to say they did not see a certain danger in earthly forms of beauty. In the thinking of some Christians, music's power to stir the emotions and draw

---

38 Lewis, *The Weight of Glory*, 31.
39 Kuyper, *De Gemeene Gratie*, 546-547 in Begbie, 97.

attention to itself is a danger indeed. As Edgar notes, "Music does have a particular power to move, and it is, therefore, to be handled with great care by those who make use of it."[40] This fear of music drawing undue attention to itself and not pointing the listener to ultimate beauty has motivated some to be wary of and even reject the use of sacred music altogether. For instance, Ulrich Zwingli feared the power of music so much that he outlawed its use in church completely.[41] John Calvin allowed the use of music in his services but restricted it to metrical Psalmody with no instrumental accompaniment. Even Augustine saw the danger of music's emotional power. His writings are replete with evidences of his struggle over whether music was beneficial for Christians:

> Thus I fluctuate between the peril of pleasure and acceptable wholesomeness. I am rather inclined, though not as if I were pronouncing an irrevocable opinion, to approve the custom of singing in the church, so that through the delight of the ears, weaker minds may rise to a feeling of devotion. Yet when it happens that I am more moved with the voice than the words sung, I confess that I have sinned.[42]

Yet it is not the pleasure itself that caused Augustine to sin, but a kind of pleasure limited to the earthly beauty only and not directed to pleasure in divine beauty. He notes, "Beauty which appeals to our senses and human imaginations (as distinguished from our intellects) is deficient."[43] Here Edwards' distinction between merely physical pleasure and "affections

---

[40] Edgar, 83.
[41] See W. P. Stephens, *Zwingli: An Introduction to His Thought* (New York: Oxford University Press, 1992), 142.
[42] Augustine, 286.
[43] Brown, 102.

of the will" will prove helpful. If certain forms of music draw a listener into a sensuous experience of physical pleasure only without deflecting its finite representation of beauty to the divine, they are not worthy of Christian use. In other words, music that merely stimulates the passions instead of uplifting the affections is dangerous.

This kind of misdirected pleasure in earthly beauty to the neglect of the divine is illustrated in the Bible as well. In the gospel accounts of Jesus Christ's transfiguration, Christ reveals some of His divine beauty in the form of "dazzling light" to three of His disciples.[44] Instead of focusing on Jesus as the manifestation of beauty, the disciples want to revel in the glory. The voice of God from heaven reprimands them, however, and admonishes them to focus on His Son.

In summary, in order for music to be enjoyed by Christians, it should redirect the observer's focus on its beauty to the source of all beauty. Music that stirs the passions alone and immodestly draws all attention to itself would not serve the process of sanctification.

A Believer's Responsibility Toward Beauty

The question, then, is what responsibility does the Christian have with regard to beauty? Are believers obligated to pursue an appreciation for what is objectively beautiful and reject those things that are ugly based upon absolute standards? Are believers expected to change their tastes?

Now in the realm of truth, believers can find explicit answers as to what is true in the Bible. The same is true for what is good. Can the same be said for beauty? The immediately

---

[44] See Matthew 17, Mark 9, and Luke 9.

apparent answer might be no, but before we settle on this answer, we need to ask how we come to know what is true and what is good in the Bible.

For instance, does the Bible explicitly tell us everything that is true? In other words, if the Bible does not say, "such and such is true," is it, therefore, false? Additionally, does the Bible explicitly tell us everything that is good? In other words, if the Bible does not say, "such and such is good," is it, therefore, evil? I think we can safely answer no to each of these questions. The Bible tells us some things that are true and some things that are good, but not everything. As pointed out in chapter 1, the Bible is our ultimate source of authority, but it is not our sole source of information. Also, it is not a textbook of prohibitions but rather a picture of God's character and desires from which we draw principles for making godly decisions. It is the responsibility of believers to use those principles that demonstrate that something is true or good and then apply them to other situations to determine their truth or goodness. This is why the Bible commands believers to exercise discernment:

Teach me good judgment and knowledge, For I believe Your commandments (Ps. 119:66).

The wise of heart is called discerning (Prov. 16:21 ESV).

Judge with righteous judgment (John 7:24).

Test all things; hold fast what is good (1 Thess. 5:21).

And know His will, and approve the things that are excellent, being instructed out of the law (Rom. 2:18).

That you may approve the things that are excellent (Phil. 1:10).

Let the others weigh what is said (1 Cor. 14:29 ESV).

Try to discern what is pleasing to the Lord (Eph. 5:10 ESV).

But solid food belongs to those who are of full age, that is, those who by reason of use have their senses exercised to discern both good and evil (Heb. 5:14).

These were more fair-minded than those in Thessalonica, in that they received the word with all readiness, and searched the Scriptures daily to find out whether these things were so (Acts 17:11).

But let each one examine his own work (Gal. 6:4).

Yes, if you cry out for discernment, And lift up your voice for understanding, If you seek her as silver, And search for her as for hidden treasures; Then you will understand the fear of the LORD, And find the knowledge of God. For the LORD gives wisdom; From His mouth come knowledge and understanding (Prov. 2:3-6).

The point of passages like these is that the Bible is not an encyclopedia of truth and goodness. It gives believers principles and examples of truth and goodness, but believers are responsible to test things and be discerning.

The same is true for beauty. Philippians 4:8 will help us here. "Finally, brothers, whatever is true, whatever is honorable, whatever is just, whatever is pure, whatever is lovely, whatever is commendable, if there is any excellence, if there is anything worthy of praise, think about these things" (ESV).

That elements of all three realms—truth, goodness, and beauty—are present in this verse is crucial in our application of this passage to our discussion. Especially notable are words like "pure," "lovely," "excellent," "praiseworthy," and especially "admirable." The Bible commands believers to think about things that are true, good, and beautiful when compared to the absolute standard of God Himself.

And that leads us back to the important question, "How do we discern what is beautiful?" I think Mortimer Adler's answer is biblically acceptable, "The judgment about the beauty of an object in terms of its admirability for intrinsic excellence or perfection is the judgment of an expert, with special knowledge and skill in judging specimens of a certain kind."[45]

Unfortunately, in the church today there is a hesitance, if not a resistance, to trust the knowledge of so-called "experts." Independence and autonomy are so highly valued that a reliance on someone else is discouraged. Insisting that someone should trust an expert is tantamount to elitism in many people's minds. Many say, "If I can't know something for myself, it is not worthy of knowing."

But if the Bible commands believers to think on those things that are actually intrinsically worthy of praise or if it commands Christians to think on those things that are demonstrably admirable, believers have one of two options. With regard to a specific question of beauty, believers can either spend the necessary time and effort to know everything there is to know about the given specimen and what makes it intrinsically beautiful, or they can trust experts who have already made the judgment.

I contend that just as believers have the biblical responsibility to pursue what is true and what is good—even in areas not explicitly addressed in Scripture—so believers must pursue what is beautiful as well. It will certainly be a continuous process of learning and growth, but it is no different in the realms

---

45 Adler, 115.

of truth and goodness. Since God's glory is His beauty, believers must look to Him as the prototype of absolute beauty, and they must be willing to recognize what is beautiful and what is ugly. Admittedly, taste is the key here. But believers are biblically responsible to sanctify their tastes when they do not correspond to reality.

For Discussion

1. Explain how God's glory is essentially His beauty.

2. Describe some of the ways the Bible ascribes beauty to God.

3. Explain why we can be certain of the existence of absolute standards for beauty.

4. Discuss how earthly beauty can point to God.

5. Discuss a believer's responsibility to pursue what is intrinsically beautiful.

CHAPTER EIGHT

Sanctifying the Emotions

Sanctification is a lifelong process for a believer. Although a Christian is freed from the power and penalty of sin, he still must deal with the presence of sin around and within him. If, as stated in 1 Corinthians 10:31, man's chief end is to glorify God, then the essence of sin is failing to accomplish this purpose. Indeed, Romans 3:23 defines sin as falling short of the glory of God. Piper's explanation of what this means will shed some light on the connection between sin and beauty:

> What does it mean to "fall short" of the glory of God? It does not mean we were supposed to be as glorious as God is and have fallen short. We ought to fall short in that sense! The best explanation of Romans 3:23 is Romans 1:23. It says that those who did not glorify or thank God "became fools, and exchanged the glory of the immortal God for images." This is the way we "fall short" of the glory of God: we exchange it for something of lesser value. All sin comes from not putting supreme value on the glory of God—this is the very essence of sin.[1]

---

[1] John Piper, *Desiring God*, 56-57.

So sin is essentially failing both to apprehend and to take pleasure in God as supreme beauty. Romans 3:10-12 emphasizes the sinfulness of men, "There is none righteous, no, not one; There is none who understands; There is none who seeks after God. They have all turned aside; They have together become unprofitable; There is none who does good, no, not one."

The London Baptist Confession correctly summarizes the doctrine of human depravity when it states that sinful man is "wholly defiled in all the faculties and parts of soul and body"[2]— that is, mind, will, and emotions. This doctrine of total depravity implies that man is completely unable to apprehend the beauty of God. When we were converted, we were given "new life" and the ability to apprehend God for who He is.

However, our sensibilities still remain partially corrupt, and the remainder of our lives on earth is occupied with sanctification, the process through which the Holy Spirit of God progressively restores the purity of man's soul—mind, will, and emotions. Thus, a Christian is constantly aware of his need to be improved and seeks, through the power of God in accordance with His Word, to progress further toward purity. The pursuit of purity includes the realm of his mind (his ability to distinguish truth from error and believe only in what is true), his will (his ability to discern right from wrong and act accordingly), and his emotions (his ability to apprehend rightly and to delight in the beauty of God). Thus, "The Christian is well aware that his tastes may be lower than his best judgment or his conscience might dictate."[3] This is a problem for the Christian, because if someone has the ability to appreciate and take pleasure only in inferior beauty, he will not be able to appreciate rightly God's superior beauty. For this reason, earthly beauty—right reflections of divine beauty—can accomplish a

---

[2] General Assembly, The Baptist Confession of Faith, 17.
[3] Kilby, 23.

sanctifying work whereby a Christian's aesthetic sensibilities are improved so he might be better equipped to apprehend and delight in God. As Augustine states, "Our whole business in this life is to restore to health the eye of the heart whereby God may be seen."[4]

For instance, if someone were to claim that a sunset were ugly, we would charge him with being dishonest and not giving proper acclaim to God's beautiful creation. People may differ on whether they prefer to watch a sunset, but to deny its beauty is to deny the beauty of God. Christians must strive to make correct judgments with regard to beauty just as they should when judging truth or goodness.

The Sanctifying Work of Beauty

The concept of the sanctifying work of beauty is common in theological writing. For instance, Herman Bavinck notes that "[beauty] deepens, broadens, and enriches our inner life, raises us momentarily above the horizontal, sinful, and sad actuality, and in a purifying, liberating, and saving manner affects our bowed and disconsolate hearts."[5] Likewise, Brown remarks, "There is something about beauty, when it is appreciated rightly, that already begins to have a kind of sanctity and that points to a higher level of reality, beautiful in itself."[6]

Furthermore, theologians have specifically linked beauty with the Holy Spirit, the person of the Trinity primarily involved with the work of sanctification. Edwards adds his voice to this subject as well. He highlights the beautifying of the world as one

---

[4] Augustine, Sermon 88.5.5, translated in Margaret Miles, "Vision: The Eye of the Body and the Eye of the Mind in Saint Augustine's De Trinitate and Confessions," *Journal of Religion* 63 (April 1983): 125-42.

[5] Herman Bavinck, "Van Schoonheid en Schoonheidsleer," chap. in Verzamelde Opstellen (Kampen: Kok, 1921), 279; quoted in Begbie, 99.

[6] Brown, 58.

of the Holy Spirit's primary functions and cites Genesis 1:2 in support, which he paraphrases as "the Spirit of God moved upon the face of the waters . . . to bring it . . . into harmony and beauty." He also quotes Job 26:13, drawing upon the Hebrew word play between "breath" and "spirit" to translate it, "God by his Spirit garnished the heavens."[7] Edwards points to sanctification as another of the Holy Spirit's primary functions, and he sees a close relationship between the two functions of sanctifying and beautifying. One statement from a sermon will summarize Edward's thinking on this point: He says that the light of the Holy Spirit, which is "a kind of emanation of God's beauty," gives a "sense of the heart" whereby Christians discover "the divine superlative glory" of God.[8] He asserts, therefore, that all true beauty can "enliven in us a sense of spiritual beauty."[9]

How this sanctifying work is accomplished through the beauty of music certainly warrants deeper investigation. To answer this, we must remember music's emotional connection. For instance, American composer Leonard Bernstein theorized that music exists as "heightened speech" and that this heightened speech is essentially "intensified emotion, . . . certainly the deepest [universal] we all share."[10] Of course, Bernstein is not the first to see a fundamental connection between music and emotion. We noted in chapter 6 that even the Bible relates music's power to its ability to express emotion.

[7] Jonathan Edwards, *An Unpublished Essay of Edwards on the Trinity, with Remarks on Edwards and His Theology*, ed. George P. Fisher (New York: C. Scribner's Sons, 1903), 90.

[8] Jonathan Edwards, "A Divine and Supernatural Light," Works, Mark Valeri, vol. 17, *Sermons and Discourses 1730-1733* (New Haven: Yale University Press, 1999), 408-26.

[9] Edwards, *The Nature of True Virtue*, 52.

[10] Bernstein, *The Unanswered Question: Six Talks at Harvard*. Cambridge, Mass.: Harvard University Press, 15.

Remember that beauty is fundamentally an emotional apprehension. Therefore, sanctifying a Christian's ability to apprehend beauty in music is essentially sanctification of his emotions. The idea of sanctifying or educating the emotions through music may seem quite remarkable. While admitting that it may sound novel, Leonard Meyer softens the blow by comparing it to educating the mind.

> It sounds perfectly reasonable to argue that reasoning can be educated in quality and depth and breadth and that we have the means to do so in education by using the forms of cognition appropriate to conceptual thinking—languages and other symbolic systems. The parallel claim being made here, that feeling can be educated in quality and depth and breadth, and that we have the means to do so in education by using the form of cognition appropriate to the affective realm—music (and the arts)—sounds remarkable or even radical.[11]

Meyer argues that this use of music to enhance the depth of what we feel is literally an "education of feeling."[12] He explains the importance of such unique education:

> If the only means available to humans to help them explore their subjective nature were ordinary language, a major part of human reality would be forever closed off to our conscious development. The subjective part of reality—the way life feels as it is lived—cannot be fully clarified or refined in our experience solely through the use of ordinary language.[13]

---

[11] Leonard B. Meyer, *Emotion and Meaning in Music* (Chicago: University of Chicago Press, 1956), 94.

[12] Ibid., 89.

[13] Ibid., 85.

Christians should be concerned to sanctify not only their minds and wills but also their emotions. Thus humans need music, and perhaps this is one of the reasons the Bible stresses the importance of music for believers. This need is further illustrated in the writing of music education specialist Bennett Reimer. He explains that our ability to articulate how we feel is limited when we use only words to describe our emotions.[14] This weakness in mere words is because "our affective experiences are seldom if ever discrete; instead, our feelings mingle and blend in countless, inseparable mixtures that the words of language cannot begin to describe because they are inherently not designed to do so."[15] The answer, according to Reimer, is that music is able to bring our feelings to "the level of awareness" by which we may "[know] through experiencing what ordinary language cannot express."

> What music does, then, is to make available for awareness, in how its organized sounds move and interrelate, the infinitely extendable, infinitely subtle, infinitely "complexifiable" possibilities of the feelings we are capable of having and so crave to have to fulfill our capacities for consciousness and cognition.[16]

In other words, music's ability to express emotion through use of symbols allows man to *know* experientially what is normally frustratingly elusive and to make value judgments about his feelings based on something external to himself. Thus man's emotions can be educated or, in religious terms, sanctified. Adler could not find any foundation for absolute "admirability" in the realm of beauty other than possibly the

---

14   Bennett Reimer, *A Philosophy of Music Education: Advancing the Vision*, third edition (Upper Saddle River, N.J.: Prentice-Hall, 2003), 84.

15   Ibid., 83.

16   Ibid., 81-2.

judgments of experts. However, he did acknowledge that the only way one could mandate taking pleasure in certain objects for their intrinsic properties is through "educational prescription."

> We think that education should result in the formation of a mind that thinks as it ought, judging correctly about the truth and falsity of propositions. We think that education should result in the formation of a virtuous moral character, one that desires aright or chooses, as it ought with regard to good and evil. To carry this one step further, from the spheres of truth and goodness to the sphere of beauty, we need only say that education should result in the formation of good taste so that the individual comes to enjoy that which is admirable, and to derive more enjoyment from objects that have greater intrinsic excellence or perfection.[17]

If Adler believed in God, he would have discovered an absolute foundation for the admirable. But the Christian has no excuse. If he is determined to have a true appreciation for divine beauty, he must be willing to cultivate and refine his tastes to appreciate the demonstrably admirable—what rightly reflects the ultimate Admirable. By exposing himself regularly to the most beautiful forms of music, a Christian can actually sanctify his emotions to appreciate true beauty. This enables him to more rightly glorify God.

How Music Can Sanctify the Emotions

The manner in which music may help to sanctify the emotions, and thus improve man's ability to rightly apprehend God's beauty, is by expressing only good, right, and wholesome

---

[17] Adler, 119.

emotions. Philosophers and theologians have always believed that music can affect human character. For instance, Plato held that music had a powerful impact upon the soul and could either ennoble people or debase them, depending upon whether the music correctly reflected universal harmony.

> Now don't we say that all music is representational and imitative? Yes . . . Then those who are looking for the best kind of singing and music must look not for the kind that is pleasant but that which is correct: and as we have said, an imitation is correct if it is made like the object imitated, both in quantity and in quality.[18]

Plato believed that since music had such a powerful potential to affect men's souls, its primary use should be for the formation of good character. He believed strongly in the use of music for the education of young people, not just academically, but spiritually.[19] Augustine also believed strongly in a distinction between objectively good and bad music and that good music could actually improve people. Faulkner notes,

> Thus Augustine conceives of music in terms of mathematics, like Plato and other Pythagoreans. This becomes even more evident in the key words that Augustine uses throughout the treatise [*De Musica*]: for example, *numerositas*, the quality that good poetry and good music exhibit, by which the hearer may perceive that they are in agreement with universal truth (i.e., cosmic harmony); or *numeri*, the various means or faculties by which humans are enabled to apprehend that harmony. (There are five of them: in the

---

[18] Plato, *Laws 668*, in Barker, *Greek Musical Writings*, vol. 1 (Cambridge: Cambridge University Press, 1984), 152.

[19] Plato, *Laws 659; 664*, in Barker, 147-148.

sound itself, in hearing, in pronouncing, in memory, and in the intellect.) Augustine indeed subscribes to the idea that music is a means of apprehending cosmic truth and perfection through the number and measure inherent in it.[20]

In Martin Luther we find perhaps the clearest articulation of how good music can sanctify. Luther knew that words alone were deficient as emotional enrichment; he needed music to encourage true piety and religious fervor. He believed that "notes bring the text to life."[21] Here he interprets Platonic thought through the eyes of Scripture and forms a basis for a theological philosophy of music. Since music can enhance the emotions and ennoble the soul, it can—when united with sound theology—provide adequate means for expressing right piety for God. "After all, the gift of language combined with the gift of song was only given to man to let him know that he should praise God with both word and music, namely, by proclaiming it through music and by providing sweet melodies with words."[22]

Luther turned to the words of the Bible for examples of music's power in this regard. The book of Psalms itself, when set to fine music, "helps greatly to produce this effect [of encouraging piety], especially when the people sing along and do so with fine devoutness."[23] Luther referenced men such as Elisha and David as biblical examples of using music to

---

[20] Quentin Faulkner, *Wiser Than Despair: The Evolution of Ideas in the Relationship of Music and the Christian Church* (Westport, Conn.: Greenwood Press, 1996), 75.

[21] *Tischreden* 2345 in Friedrich Blume, et al, *Protestant Church Music: A History* (New York: W. W. Norton & Company, 1974), 14.

[22] Helmut T. Lehmann, ed. *Luther's Works*, vol. 3 (Philadelphia: Fortress, 1965), 321-324.

[23] Edwald M. Plass, gen. ed., *What Luther Says*, vol. 2 (Saint Louis: Concordia, 1959), 981.

enrich the emotions.[24] Luther's sermons and other writings are replete with advice to use music as a means to encourage right emotions such as "a calm and joyful disposition."[25] To an organist in Freiberg, Luther wrote,

> When you are sad, say to yourself, "Come! I will strike up a song to my Lord Jesus Christ on the regal, be it Te Deum Laudamus or Benedictus, for the Scriptures teach me that He rejoices in glad song and the sound of strings." So with renewed spirit reach for the claves and sing until your sad thoughts are driven away, as did David and Elisha.[26]

This kind of emotional enrichment drew Martin Luther to relish fine music for use in the church, because he saw music as a gift from heaven, "an endowment of God, not a gift of men,"[27] to be used "in the service of him who has given and created [it]."[28] Luther had no patience for those who would not submit themselves to the benefits of musical enrichment for the betterment of the soul. He called them "stumps and blocks of stone."[29]

In Luther's mind, this power of music to stimulate right emotions and elevate the soul created better people. Luther noted that good music developed "people of wondrous ability, subsequently fit for everything," for "he who knows music has a good nature."[30] That is why he believed so strongly that young people should be educated in music, so they "might

[24] 2 Kings 3:15; 2 Sam. 1:17ff; See Paul Nettle, *Luther and Music* (New York: Russell & Russell, 1967), 16.
[25] Lehmann, vol. 49, 427.
[26] Nettle, 16.
[27] Plass, 980.
[28] Martin Luther, *Works: Spiritual Hymn Book*, vol. 6, 284.
[29] Lehmann, *Luther's Works*, vol. 49, 427-429.
[30] Ibid., vol. 45, 369-370; Plass, 980.

have something whereby [they] might be weaned from the love ballads and the sex songs and, instead of these, learn something beneficial and take up the good with relish, as benefits youth."[31] Luther wanted good people, rightly conformed to the teachings of Scripture in knowledge and affection, and he found in music the perfect gift from God for this task.

In summary, only well-crafted music, because it is demonstrably beautiful, can educate the emotions and ennoble character. It can do so exactly because good creations of beauty are a reflection of divine beauty and help to cleanse sinful affections and make one more able to appreciate what he should. Plato's philosophy presents a clue as to how this sanctification takes place. He insisted that music be not merely "pleasant" but "correct," and by correct he means that it must correspond rightly to "cosmic harmony."[32] The Christian interpretation of such thinking is found in Augustine who tied that "cosmic truth" with God's perfections.[33] And so it is to the cosmos—nature—that a Christian must look if he is to rightly represent divine beauty. I have shown that creation itself is beautiful in that it comes from the hand of Beauty Himself, and so, as Kilby notes, man-made "art may rightly take its cue from God's own practice, for He tells us that the heavens declare his glory."[34] In studying the beauty of creation and attempting to mimic its qualities in art such as music, a Christian may educate his tastes and prepare himself to be able to apprehend the beauty of God. Sherry summarizes this notion well:

---

[31] Plass, 980-981.
[32] Plato, in Barker, 152.
[33] Faulkner, 75.
[34] Kilby, 30.

In the case of aesthetics, Christian theologians, and indeed all theists, start from the assumption that the beautiful aspects of nature are properties put there by God as creator of all things (which is not to deny that beauty may be supervenient on other qualities); they may be led from there to explore the footsteps of the Creator, through scientific investigation as well as contemplation of nature and artistic activity, and to rejoice in his creation; many have gone further and seen the beauty of works of art too as created by God, though in this case indirectly, through his inspiration of artists as "secondary causes"; and many see both natural and artistic beauty as a reflection of, or likeness to, God's own beauty.[35]

So what, then, are those qualities that render music well crafted? What are those properties in nature that reveal God's perfections of beauty—those qualities that composers should imitate if they want to create truly beautiful music as reflections of the divine or those qualities that the Christian listener should look for? For the answer to these questions, we must return to an observation of the qualities of perfection in the character of God and the beauty in His creation. A synthesis of the writings of men like Edwards, Kuyper, Aquinas, and Augustine will reveal three overarching categories of properties that render both God and His creation beautiful: (1) order (unity, regularity, harmony, uniformity, etc.), (2) proportion (symmetry and balance, etc.), and (3) radiance (effulgence, purity, clarity, etc.). Each of these qualities is used in Scripture to describe God.

---

[35] Sherry, 47.

Likewise, God makes aesthetic judgments about His creation or man-made art based on the same qualities. Recognition of such qualities should be significant for a Christian since failure to recognize these properties as those that comprise the beauty of God is to fail to bring Him the glory due Him. Furthermore, to call something beautiful or take aesthetic delight in something that does not possess these qualities reflective of God's beauty is tantamount to sin. Therefore, if a Christian wants to glorify God and magnify His excellence by true beauty in music, he must reflect these properties of divine beauty—order, proportion, and radiance—in his craft. No magical formula exists to help the Christian evaluate music based on these criteria—this is the task of informed musical analysis. But all Christians must be willing to do the study necessary to understand what makes good music from an analytical standpoint and make decisions accordingly.

In summary, music has three primary functions: (1) By taking delight in those properties of music that mimic God's perfections and thus making it beautiful, the listener affirms God's beauty, bringing ultimate glory to Him; (2) Since every man is born seeking pleasure, finite pleasure gives the listener a small taste of what may be fully consummated only in God. This motivates the listener to seek after God, the source of true delight; and (3) Truly beautiful music can educate the listener's emotions and help him grow to have a full appreciation for what deserves admiration, including God Himself.

For Discussion

1. In what ways might our emotions need sanctifying?

2. Explain how music can sanctify the emotions.

3. How can we know whether something is truly beautiful and will, therefore, help in sanctifying the emotions?

4. What are some observable qualities that reveal true beauty?

CHAPTER NINE

Making Musical Choices

Thus far we have established that all of life should be lived as a response of worship to truth we know about God. We have studied the doctrine of sanctification and shown it to be an active life of pursing godliness and determining what will help us and others become more holy. Since music carries meaning to the emotions, and since our affections link what we believe to how we live, it is important that we guard what is influencing our affections, especially music. And since music that reflects God's character through its beauty glorifies Him, Christians should strive to love only what is truly beautiful.

Now we move to more specific applications of these biblical principles to the issue of music in everyday life. How do we make right decisions? How do we combine principles from Scripture with other information about music that we have discovered?

Texts: the Black and White Issue

When discussing musical styles, it is often the music itself that is the issue at hand. Since musical style is not specifically addressed in Scripture, it is understandable that this would be a controversial issue.

The texts of music, however, should not be controversial. The Bible is clear concerning what pleases the Lord in this area. It is unfortunate that many Christians are not careful about the texts they approve. Content with mediocre Christianity and not actively pursuing godliness, many believers tolerate clearly unbiblical music in their lives.

Corrupt Communication

> Let no corrupt word proceed out of your mouth, but what is good for necessary edification, that it may impart grace to the hearers (Eph. 4:29).

The Bible is very clear that Christians are not to let any unwholesome talk come out of their mouths. The words of songs, therefore, must not contain corrupt communication. What is corrupt communication? Here are some biblical examples:

> Flee sexual immorality. Every sin that a man does is outside the body, but he who commits sexual immorality sins against his own body (1 Cor. 6:18).

> Now the works of the flesh are evident, which are: adultery, fornication, uncleanness, lewdness, idolatry, sorcery, hatred, contentions, jealousies, outbursts of wrath, selfish ambitions, dissensions, heresies, envy, murders, drunkenness, revelries, and the like; of which I tell you beforehand, just as I also told you in time past, that those who practice such things will not inherit the kingdom of God (Gal. 5:19-21).

> But fornication and all uncleanness or covetousness, let it not even be named among you, as is fitting for saints; neither filthiness, nor foolish talking, nor coarse jesting, which are not fitting, but rather giving of thanks. For this you know, that no

fornicator, unclean person, nor covetous man, who is an idola-
ter, has any inheritance in the kingdom of Christ and God.
Let no one deceive you with empty words, for because of these
things the wrath of God comes upon the sons of disobedi-
ence. Therefore do not be partakers with them (Eph. 5:3-7).

But now you yourselves are to put off all these: anger,
wrath, malice, blasphemy, filthy language out of your mouth
(Col. 3:8).

Any song text that comes close to discussing or promoting
any of these sinful acts is certainly unacceptable for a believer.
That should be an obvious and easily obeyed truth, but unfortunately, many believers fail miserably in this very clear, direct
area. No Christian can expect to determine what kind of music
style he should listen to if he is not willing first to remove from
his life music with clearly sinful texts.

What Is Good for Edification

Instead of these sinful subjects, good texts will have content
that is edifying and building—that which fits the Philippians 4:8
model: "Finally, brethren, whatever things are true, whatever
things are noble, whatever things are just, whatever things are
pure, whatever things are lovely, whatever things are of good
report, if there is any virtue and if there is anything praiseworthy—meditate on these things."

Music: the "Foggy" Issue

As I have already noted, for the music itself (as well as
many other issues in the Christian life), God does not give us a
list of what pleases Him and what does not please Him. Some
may try to insist that it is a black and white issue. They may say

that only sacred music is pleasing to God or only songs sung in unison or without instrumental accompaniment. They want to make music a black and white issue with a clear line of distinction between what is good and what is bad. It is not that simple, however.

An important issue in determining what music pleases the Lord is whether music carries meaning that influences morality. This point was considered in chapter 6. We discovered that both scriptural evidence and common human experience prove that music communicates general moods universally. It does so by accurately reflecting the natural expressions of the emotions it communicates. This is important because we must admit that there could be such a thing as good and bad music, based upon whether what it communicates could be pleasing or displeasing to the Lord.

Seeing Through the Fog

It would be nice if the issue of musical style were as simple as evaluating what it communicates and deciding whether it is acceptable to the Lord. It is not, however, that simple. Human finiteness and depravity hinder us from easily determining such things. It would be nice if music were a black and white issue with a clear line distinguishing bad music from good music. Unfortunately, it is not that easy. We must affirm, however, that this is the case in the mind of God. In His mind there is a line. In other words, there is no such thing as neutral music. Any given song is either good or evil. To deny such a truth would be to deny absolutes. Absolute truth in this area does exit; the problem arises from man's finiteness.

Some people will admit there is clearly bad music and clearly good music, but they insist that there is a middle *gray* area that is neutral. That cannot be true, however. We have already noted that music communicates universal moods. There is no such thing as music that communicates nothing. Consequently, we must affirm that God has a definite line in His mind separating good music from evil music. It is because of our creatureliness and sinfulness that we cannot see the line that God has set regarding music. He has not chosen to delineate it for us, and, therefore, we do not know where it is.

So where does this leave us? What do we do with this middle area? Instead of viewing the middle foggy area as neutral, we should recognize that music is on a continuum from bad to good. The middle foggy area is not neutral; it is progressing slowly and almost unnoticeably from bad to good. In the mind of God there is a line somewhere in the middle. But though we affirm that there is definitely bad and good music and no such thing as "neutral," we cannot always determine where good becomes bad.

This fact can be easily illustrated. For instance, what is a pile of sand? Is it one grain or five grains or 50 grains? While recognizing a pile of sand is easy, determining exactly when it becomes a pile of sand is difficult. Or when does fall become winter? Is it when the temperature reaches 30? What if the next day it is 65 again? Recognizing winter is easy, while the hard part is determining when the change between fall and winter takes place. Or when is the moment when I need a haircut? We could never pinpoint the second when my hair becomes long, but it is easy to recognize when I need a haircut.

Here's another example from a science experiment. A frog was placed in a pot of water on a stove. The temperature of the stove was raised very slowly over a period of time. The frog didn't notice the change and peacefully boiled to death. The frog never noticed the point at which his environment became dangerous to him. But the fact that the scientists enjoyed frog legs proves that, at some point, it did become dangerous!

One final illustration. In 1964 the United States Supreme Court heard a case regarding censorship of pornography. The difficulty they found was agreeing upon a settled definition of what pornography is. Justice Potter Stewart wrote that he "perhaps could never succeed in intelligibly" explaining what it is. "But I know it when I see it."[1]

The point is: Recognizing clearly immoral music is fairly easy—any Christian can do it. Trying to determine where the line between good and bad music is, however, remains difficult, if not impossible for finite man. Therefore, staying away from the middle may be prudent for the Christian.

Making Choices that Glorify God

So how, then, do we make musical choices based on all of this information? When we combine biblical principles of decision-making and sanctification with truths about how music communicates, we can come to some biblical decisions in this area of music.

Reject music that clearly communicates unwholesome messages.

Some music clearly communicates sinful messages. Christians should certainly stay clear of such music. Sometimes an honest view of history or an evaluation of current associations with a certain style of music can be helpful in this regard. If, in times past or in the present, a certain music style is associated with or used by ungodly movements or causes, there may be good reason to deduce that the music communicates messages that are compatible with their sinful message. Associa-

---

[1] Paul Gerwirtz, "On 'I Know It When I See It,'" *Yale Law Journal*, Vol. 15 (1996), 1023-1047.

tions do not make the music sinful, but they are often simply shadows of reality.

Often unbelievers are more honest about what their music communicates than believers are. For instance, most rock musicians are quick to admit that their music communicates messages such as rebellion and unbridled sexuality:

> Heavy metal's main subject matter is simple and virtually universal. It celebrates teen-agers' newfound feeling of rebellion and sexuality (Jon Pareles, music critic).[2]

> I've always thought that the main ingredients in rock are sex, really good stage shows and really sassy music. Sex and sass, I really think that's where it's at (Debbie Harry, lead singer of the Blondies).[3]

> Rock 'n' roll is 99% sex (John Oates of Hall and Oates).[4]

> Rock music is sex. The big beat matches the body's rhythms (Frank Zappa).[5]

> The throbbing beat of rock-and-roll provides a vital sexual release for its adolescent audience (Jan Berry of Jan and Dean).[6]

> Our music is, and always has been, fueled by a strong sexual undertow. Pop music is partially about sex. The two things can't be divorced (Neil Tennant of the Pet Shop Boys).[7]

---

[2] Jon Pareles, "Metallica Defies Heavy Metal Stereotypes," *Minneapolis Star Tribune*, 13 July 1988, 12 Ew.

[3] *Hit Parader*, September 1979, quoted in John Blanchard, Peter Anderson, and Derek Cleave, *Pop Goes the Gospel* (Welwyn, England: Evangelical Press, 1983), 32.

[4] Circus, 31.1.76 in Blanchard, 41.

[5] David A. Noebel, *Christian Rock: A Stategem of Mephistopheles*. Manitou Springs, Colo.: Summit Ministries, n.d., 6.

[6] Blanchard et al., 44.

[7] Stan Hawkins, "The Pet Shop Boys: Musicology, Masculinity and Banality," in *Sexing the Groove: Popular Music and Gender*, ed. Sheila Whiteley (New York: Routledge, 1997), 124.

Obviously, we must take these very blunt and honest statements into account when we evaluate rock music styles. They do not *make* rock music wrong, but it would be naive to ignore them. This same practice could be applied to all genres of music. Even the texts of many pop songs testify to the fact that certain musical forms are intrinsically sexual. For instance, in the lyrics to "Turn the Beat Around," Gerald Jackson and Peter Jackson readily admit that the rhythms encourage sexual movement. Similarly, in "Rhythm is Gonna Get You," Gloria Estefan recites the almost hypnotic power of her rhythm. These lyrics are honest about what the music means and what it targets. We would be foolish to ignore them.

Ask honest questions about what the music communicates.

After we have eliminated music that is clearly displeasing to the Lord, we must then ask honest questions about what the music communicates. We must be willing to evaluate the music based upon standards outside ourselves. We must set aside our tastes and preferences and ask, "What does this music say?" If we find that it communicates messages that are sinful or even hint at sin, we must reject the music. Again, looking at associations and common responses to the music will help.

Apply biblical principles and make decisions that glorify God.

Once we have eliminated clearly wrong music and asked all the right questions, we must take one more step. Remember, sanctification is an active pursuit of godliness, so we are not asking the question, "What's wrong with this music?" but "What's right with this music?" Let's apply the principles we found in chapter 3 specifically to music.

Is the music beneficial? The question is not does this music harm you, but does this music help you? Does it aid your spiritual growth? Does it make you a better person? Is your walk with the Lord stronger as a result of the music?

Does the music risk failing to bring God glory? If music is a continuum progressing almost imperceptibly from good music to bad, we should strive to stay as far from the line as possible. Unfortunately, many people are constantly trying to see how close to the edge they can get without moving into sin. Dedicated believers who are concerned primarily with the glory of God will not risk failing to bring God glory.

Does the music offend others? If a particular genre of music causes a significant number of people to stumble, especially if that includes people you know and trust, then that is a good reason to be wary of the music. Paul says in such cases you have the freedom to give up such music.

Does the music control you? So many people cling to *their* music because they love it, and in reality, are controlled by it. Yet that is one very important reason that Paul was willing to give things up. He said that being fundamentally controlled by things could be damning! People are often unwilling to get rid of a certain kind of music because it is *their* music. Yet that is exactly what Paul warned against. If any kind of music controls us, we must get rid of it.

Making decisions regarding music is no different than making decisions in any other area of the Christian life. If a person is genuinely concerned with his sanctification; if he is willing to ask the right questions and give up what he is not certain will please the Lord; if he is daily in God's Word, striving to know more about God and think more like God; he will certainly glorify God with his music.

For Discussion

1. What are some subjects of pop songs that are clearly "unwholesome communication" but that some Christians overlook?

2. How can observing associations with various musical styles help in determining intrinsic meaning?

3. What kinds of common reactions to certain music might reveal that it communicates unwholesome meaning?

4. What biblical principles should guide a believer in determining the kind of music he should listen to?

5. List some music that may cause others to stumble into sin.

Conclusion

The Bible is clear that a true Christian will progress in holiness—it is inevitable. But while sanctification is inevitable, it is not automatic. A believer must work diligently to progress in righteousness, and consistent application of the Bible to his life is key. But a Christian must not be satisfied with only obeying explicit commands and avoiding explicit prohibitions. As we noted in chapter 1, the Bible is not an encyclopedia of commands and prohibitions, but a window into the mind and heart of God.

Therefore, it is incumbent upon all Christians to actively apply biblical principles to every area of their lives, whether or not particular issues are addressed specifically in Scripture.

That certainly applies to the music they enjoy as well. The Bible does not specifically address what kind of music is appropriate for believers to enjoy. But the Bible is replete with principles that can—no, must—be applied to the music we listen to and perform. Since music is a form of communication, all principles regarding communication apply. Because music targets the affections, and because our affection for the Lord is the essence of true Christianity, we must be very careful what we allow to shape our affections. Since God is supreme Beauty and the source of all earthly beauty, we must learn to love only those things that are truly beautiful.

In May 2004, filmmaker Morgan Spurlock released a film documenting his experience of eating only fast food for a month. During that period Spurlock gained 24 pounds, his cholesterol skyrocketed, and even his moods were affected.

Any parent who is concerned with the physical well being of his child will not allow the child to eat junk food on a regular basis. Fast foods and sweets certainly are not lethal—they are not poisonous—but they are certainly not healthful, and a steady diet of such foods will have debilitating effects.

Music is not too different. Music exists on a continuum from bad to good. Somewhere in the middle there is a line, but it is difficult for men to delineate it. However, the further from the middle toward the good side, the better the music. Music closer to the middle may not be inherently wrong—it is not sinful—but it is certainly not healthful, and a steady diet of such music will have debilitating effects.

How do we know that junk food is unhealthful? We trust experts and observe its general characteristics and side effects. We would be foolish to ignore warnings against ingesting cyanide just because the Bible doesn't tell us not to eat it. We must be willing to do the same with regard to music.

Determine to be active, not passive, in your musical choices. Decide to listen only to the kinds of music that clearly glorify God—that music that helps your spiritual growth, ennobles your affections, and teaches you to love what is beautiful.

For Discussion

1. How has your understanding of the purpose of the Bible in a believer's life changed since you started reading this book?

2. In what ways do your emotions need to be sanctified?

3. List some music that you regularly listen to that might actually be debasing your emotions rather than ennobling them.

4. List some music that you regularly listen to that sanctifies your emotions.

5. In what other ways has your thinking been changed as a result of this book so far?

SECTION III

Music in Assembled Worship

CHAPTER TEN

Worshiping God in the Assembly

In section 2 we discussed music and worship in general but did not narrow the topic to congregational worship specifically. From this point on, however, the focus of this book will be precisely that—congregational worship.

Three Biblical "Styles" of Worship

There is a lot of discussion by Christians about different "worship styles" and whether they please the Lord. Terms such as "conservative," "traditional," "contemporary," and "blended" are used to describe differing philosophies of worship style. Scripture reveals three definite biblical worship styles.

Lifestyle Worship

The first style of worship was considered in chapter 2: All of life should be worship. Every decision a person makes should be a response to truth. That is best expressed in passages such as 1 Corinthians 10:31 and Romans 12:1:

> Therefore, whether you eat or drink, or whatever you do, do all to the glory of God (1 Cor. 10:31).

I beseech you therefore, brethren, by the mercies of God, that you present your bodies a living sacrifice, holy, acceptable to God, which is your reasonable service (Rom. 12:1).

All of a believer's life should be for God's glory. That is the essence of worship. As we continually present our lives to God, we are worshiping Him. Progressively becoming like Christ is one of the best ways of magnifying His unique excellence. In this sense, all of life is designed to be worship. When we understand those attributes unique to God and seek to magnify them through our actions, we are worshiping God with our response to truth. We were created to worship God in that way. We should also note that the "therefore" in Romans 12:1 indicates this response of worship flows from the truth about God expressed in the first eleven chapters of Romans. So even in "lifestyle worship," both truth about God and the believer's response must be present.

As a Christian progresses in his sanctification, he learns more truth from God's Word. He should respond to that truth by changing anything that does not conform to Scripture and rejoicing in the rich truths he has learned. That, of course, necessitates his diligent study of the Bible and being under sound preaching. That also necessitates striving to understand truth.

Private Worship

A more narrowed style of worship is private worship—when a Christian spends dedicated personal time with the Lord in His Word and in prayer. As a believer studies the Word of God, the Holy Spirit will illumine him as to the significance of that Scripture to his life, and he should respond accordingly. Private worship is a very individual, intimate form of worship, and the worshiper's responses will reflect this intimacy. Here the truth about God is very personal; it is directed to a specific individual. The believer's response will also be very personal and unique to his situation. There are several examples in Scripture of those who set apart specific and definite times to worship God.

David said, "My voice You shall hear in the morning, O LORD; In the morning I will direct it to You, And I will look up" (Ps. 5:3) and later, "Seven times a day I praise You, Because of Your righteous judgments" (Ps. 119:164).

Now when Daniel knew that the writing was signed, he went home. And in his upper room, with his windows open toward Jerusalem, he knelt down on his knees three times that day, and prayed and gave thanks before his God, as was his custom since early days (Dan. 6:10).

Now in the morning, having risen a long while before daylight, [Jesus] went out and departed to a solitary place; and there He prayed (Mark 1:35).

Private worship is a vital and necessary part of every believer's life. No Christian can please God without it. Believers must diligently study God's Word and then respond to the truth through heartfelt prayer, confession, and affection for God.

Congregational Worship

The third style of worship is congregational worship—the gathering of the people of God to worship Him corporately. Scripture clearly commands and exemplifies this form of worship:

Praise the LORD! I will praise the LORD with my whole heart, In the assembly of the upright and in the congregation (Ps. 111:1).

Praise the LORD! Sing to the LORD a new song, And His praise in the assembly of saints (Ps. 149:1).

In these passages, the psalmist exhorts the believer to praise Jehovah and to do so in the assembly of believers. Old Testament believers recognized the importance of worshiping congregationally, and the practice carried over into the New Testament church as well. The Bible commands New Testament believers to gather together on a regular basis. First Corinthians 14:23 speaks of the whole church gathering together. Acts 2:46 tells of the early church attending the temple together and breaking bread in their homes. Hebrews 10:25 commands believers not to neglect meeting together. Although there is no explicit statement that the purpose for these meetings was congregational worship, there are several reasons we can be sure that worship did occur.

First, early Christian gatherings naturally included many Jewish worship practices. Andrew Hill, an Old Testament scholar, argues, "It is only natural . . . that we seek the origins of early Christian worship in Jewish temple and synagogue worship."[1]

Second, it is clear from New Testament narratives that what took place at gatherings of the church included acts of congregational worship:

> And they continued steadfastly in the apostles' doctrine and fellowship, in the breaking of bread, and in prayers. Then fear came upon every soul, and many wonders and signs were done through the apostles. Now all who believed were together, and had all things in common, and sold their possessions and goods, and divided them among all, as anyone had need. So continuing daily with one accord

---

[1] Hill, 222.

in the temple, and breaking bread from house to house, they ate their food with gladness and simplicity of heart, praising God and having favor with all the people. And the Lord added to the church daily those who were being saved (Acts 2:42-47).

Now in the church that was at Antioch there were certain prophets and teachers: Barnabas, Simeon who was called Niger, Lucius of Cyrene, Manaen who had been brought up with Herod the tetrarch, and Saul. As they ministered to the Lord and fasted… (Acts 13:1-2).

Also, the New Testament describes gatherings of believers as the temple of God. The Elizabethan English of the King James Version of the Bible readily reveals the plural pronouns used when Old Testament Temple language is used to describe the Church:

Now therefore ye [plural pronoun, "you all" as a local church congregation] are no more strangers and foreigners, but fellow citizens with the saints, and of the household of God; And are built upon the foundation of the apostles and prophets, Jesus Christ himself being the chief corner stone; In whom all the building fitly framed together groweth unto an *holy temple* [naos, same word used for the Holy Place in the Temple] in the Lord: In whom ye also are builded together for an *habitation of God* through the Spirit (Eph. 2:19-22 KJV, emphasis added).

For we are labourers together with God: ye [plural pronoun] are God's husbandry, ye are *God's building* [oikos, "dwelling"] (1 Cor. 3:9 KJV, emphasis added).

Know ye [plural pronoun] not that ye are the *temple* [*naos*] of God, and that the Spirit of God dwelleth in you [plural]? If any man defile the temple of God, him shall God destroy; for the temple of God is holy, which *temple* ye [plural] are (1 Cor. 3:16-17 KJV emphasis added).

Ye [plural pronoun] also, as lively stones, are built up a *spiritual house* [*oikos*], an holy priesthood, to offer up spiritual sacrifices, acceptable to God by Jesus Christ. But ye are a chosen generation, a royal priesthood, an holy nation, a peculiar people; that ye should shew forth the praises of him who hath called you out of darkness into his marvellous light (1 Peter 2:5, 9 KJV emphasis added).

Both Old Testament command and New Testament example demonstrate that God desires that believers lift His praises together. He wants His children to gather for the purpose of honoring Him. This worship is still an individual, heartfelt response toward God, but it is expressed publicly in the presence of other believers. That brings God even more glory than if it were done privately.

For instance, a person receives more honor when he is praised in the presence of many people than if he were praised by one person privately. The great honor that comes with winning an Olympic gold medal is because thousands of people are watching the event. A solo violin can be beautiful, but when it is combined with other instruments in a symphony, the glory of the music is even more spectacular. The same is true when God is praised publicly in the presence of others. C. H. Spurgeon said, "Personal praise is sweet unto God, but congregational praise has a multiplicity of sweetnesses in it."[2]

---

[2] C. H. Spurgeon, "Psalm the Hundred and Forty-Ninth" in *The Treasury of David*, Vol. IV: *Psalms 90-103* (Grand Rapids: Baker Book House), 438.

Therefore, congregational worship could be defined as *a unified chorus of spiritual responses toward God expressed publicly to God, as a result of understanding biblical truth about God.*

Though the three styles of worship are distinct, they are interrelated. They must all be present in a believer's life. Without private and congregational worship, a believer will not worship God with his lifestyle. If believers do not worship God throughout the week privately and with their lives, congregational worship will be dead and meaningless. If a Christian isn't consistently faithful in congregational worship, he will not worship the Lord in other areas.

Another important factor is that with each different style of worship, both the content of the worship and the response toward God will be slightly different. With lifestyle worship, the content is a person's experiences of what God has done, interpreted through his understanding of biblical truth, and the response will be obedience and Christ-likeness. With private worship, the content will be the Word of God as it is applied to a person's life individually, and the response will be very personal and intimate. With congregational worship, the content will be God's revelation given to the whole congregation, and the response will be unified and corporate.

Congregational Worship Music: Narrowed by Purpose

It is often easy to blend and confuse the issues of sacred music and secular music (whether pop or classical) when discussing general music philosophy. It is sometimes unclear whether someone who is attempting to establish a biblical philosophy of music is discussing general principles applicable to all music or specific principles that address sacred music alone.

155

It is important to make clear distinctions between lifestyle worship and congregational worship. In chapter 2 we saw that all of life is worship. Principles set forth in sections 1 and 2 will help us make music decisions as lifestyle worship decisions. Section 3 narrows our discussion to congregational worship, and it is necessary to do so with regard to music as well. Just as the criteria for congregational worship are more narrowed than for lifestyle worship because of its purpose, so congregational worship music must be focused.

First we start very broadly. Music, generally speaking, is any sound that is organized in such a way that it communicates to people. It can be anything from a simple child's song to a complex symphony. Believers can worship the Lord with their lifestyles as they choose music that is pleasing to Him. General principles of Christian conduct, such as those explored in section 1, should govern this broadest category of music.

Sacred music, more narrowed, is music that communicates a message that is specifically biblical. This could include music that is addressed to God or other believers. Believers can use this kind of music in their private worship or generally throughout their week. The music may be a personal or intimate expression of an individual's worship to God. Because biblical truth is being supported with such music, standards for this music should be stricter than for music in general.

The narrowest kind of music is sacred music that is specifically designed for congregational worship. This is music that is either addressed to God or expresses truth about God that is applicable for all believers. Some music expresses truth that may not be true for all believers, a type of music that does not fit in this category. Nor is music appropriate that is very intimate or that expresses only individual adoration to God.

The purpose of congregational worship is corporate response, and the music used should reflect this.

Why is that so? Why must music used in congregational worship be so focused and narrow? We defined congregational worship as *a unified chorus of spiritual responses toward God expressed publicly to God as a result of understanding biblical truth about God.* From this biblical definition, we can determine what the necessary characteristics of congregational worship music should be. But first, we must ask the question: "Why do we even have music in congregational worship at all?"

For Discussion

1. Discuss reasons that congregational worship is unique and distinct from lifestyle worship.

2. Discuss biblical evidence that the early church gathered for the purpose of corporate worship.

3. Describe the different terms connected with Old Testament worship that are used in the New Testament to designate the church.

4. Explain why the content of congregational worship will necessarily be narrowed from lifestyle worship.

CHAPTER ELEVEN

Why Do We Need Sacred Music?

This may seem like an odd question. Most, if not all, churches have music, don't they? That is just how it has always been, right?

While this may seem like an odd question, I believe it is an important issue to discuss because of the myriads of faulty answers people give. For instance, I have heard some say the music of a worship service is simply a prelude to the preaching. Those people view music as nonessential to a worship service. We could eliminate it altogether, and they wouldn't miss it at all. Others say that music "sets the mood" for the preaching. That is still a "prelude to preaching" type of thinking, although these people would probably agree that music is a good thing because it does "prepare our hearts" for the message. A third group—and this is what I've heard more often—say the reason we have music in churches is so we can teach and affirm biblical truth. That answer may sound a bit better, but I insist it is no better an answer than the other two.

The reason these answers are faulty is that they completely miss the primary reason for music in church. They focus only on the words of music in the church and give no thought to the

159

actual music itself or even to the poetic form of the words. You can recognize a person with that kind of reasoning because, when they evaluate music for use in the church, the only question they ask is, "Are the words biblical?" That is a great question, but it is not enough. The purpose for music in the church goes beyond just the words. The reason we have music involves more than just a nice setting for teaching and affirming biblical truth.

What Is the Purpose of the Church?

To answer the question of why we have music in church, we must first ask questions about the purposes of the church in general. The Bible gives the church specific missions to fulfill, and if the church engages in any activity that does not support its mission, that activity should be eliminated.

To Establish Mature Followers of Christ

With specific reference to believers, churches are responsible to establish mature followers of Christ. Ephesians 4:11-16 best demonstrates this mission of the church.

And He Himself gave some to be apostles, some prophets, some evangelists, and some pastors and teachers, for the equipping of the saints for the work of ministry, for the edifying of the body of Christ, till we all come to the unity of the faith and of the knowledge of the Son of God, to a perfect man, to the measure of the stature of the fullness of Christ; that we should no longer be children, tossed to and fro and carried about with every wind of doctrine, by the trickery of men, in the cunning craftiness of deceitful plotting, but, speaking the truth in love, may grow up in all things into Him who is the head—Christ—from whom the whole body, joined and knit together by what every joint supplies, according to the effective working by which every part does its share, causes growth of the body for the edifying of itself in love.

How does a church accomplish the goal of maturing believers? Simply stated, the church accomplishes it by encouraging its members to follow the Bible. Through various means, Christians become more mature as they submit to biblical directives. What is important, however, is that the church aim for the whole of man to obey all of God's commands. Every part of man must be matured. In the Bible, God addresses what we think, what we do, and how we feel—mind, will, and emotions. As we noted in chapter 4, it is no better illustrated than in the great Hebrew confession of faith in Deuteronomy 6:4-6: "Hear, O Israel: The Lord our God, the Lord is one! You shall love the Lord your God with all your heart, with all your soul, and with all your strength. And these words which I command you today shall be in your heart."

God addressed all three parts of man. He first addressed what they must believe in their minds: God is one and He is Yahweh. He then addressed their emotions: They are to love that God. And finally, he addressed their wills: They must obey that God. The rest of Scripture deals the same way with man— his mind, will, and emotions are to fall under the rule of God. All three work together for a person to glorify God: doctrine, action, and affection. So if a church is to establish mature followers of Christ who declare His excellencies, it must aim to improve the whole of man: his beliefs, his actions, and his emotions. That is the duty of everyone in the congregation, and especially the leadership.

To Declare God's Excellencies in Corporate Worship

Before we discuss how a church might accomplish this maturing, let us focus specifically on the purpose of a church in its congregational worship. Our Lord said in John 4 that God desires people who worship in "spirit and truth." As we noted in chapter 2, He was contrasting the common religious thought of the day that said that worship had to be done in certain outward forms in specific locations. Christ emphasized that true worship is inward responses to biblical truth. That response to truth can take the form of action or affection. So here again we have all three elements of man that congregational worship must address: truth, morality (action), and right affection (spirit).

We must also note that these three elements of man are intricately connected. The Bible does not separate the three. Anything that is biblically true is, therefore, good because it comes from God, and it should stir the affections. We must love righteousness that is based on truth. And our affections must be based on truth and goodness. We cannot separate the three.

The Means to Establish Mature Followers of Christ

How does a church accomplish its mission of establishing mature followers of Christ? Let us look at each of the three elements we've discussed, keeping in mind that they are interconnected.

First, a church helps to mature the mind primarily through biblical teaching. This can be in a formal Bible class, Sunday School, training times, or weekly preaching. We cannot make too much of consistent biblical teaching that aims at shaping what believers think and believe. Therefore, maturing the mind is accomplished primarily through words.

Second, a church helps to mature the will by applying biblical principles and through exhortation. As the Word of God is taught, a pastor will admonish believers to follow what it says and change if they do not conform to its teaching. A church that emphasizes truth but neglects application of that truth in holiness and conformity to God's commands is negligent. Therefore, maturing the will, too, is accomplished primarily through words.

Most good churches strive to accomplish these two goals. We make much of doctrine, and we make much of holiness. However, it is the third element of man that many have failed to consider carefully.

How does a church help to mature believers' emotions? Certainly truth and righteousness are at the root of biblical affections, so the use of words through teaching and preaching does help to mature believers' emotions as well. But emotion simply cannot be adequately put into words. If I want to tell you what you should believe, I will use words. If I want to tell you how you should act, I will use words. But if I want to tell you how you should feel, words are inadequate. Furthermore, words are not only incapable of telling you how you should feel, but they are also inadequate as expressions of how you feel. Any husband knows what it is to be unable to express adequately with words the love he has for his wife. No wife is satisfied with an occasional, "I love you." Words alone are not enough to express what can better be expressed by other means. Sometimes a look or a touch does more to express heartfelt affection than any words can. That is why we have love poems; they help to express love in a way that cannot be expressed with just words, for poetry is an art form that takes the words to the heart. Likewise, Christians need another language than just words both to prescribe the affections they should have for God and describe the affections they do have for God.

That other language is music.

Using Music to Mature the Emotions

If churches want to establish mature believers, they must aim at the whole of man, including his emotions. God has given music to man as a tool to help him express his emotions. That point was thoroughly explained in chapter 6, but it deserves specific application to church music here. Any casual reader of Scripture will recognize the clear connection between music and sacred emotional expression. Here are just a few examples:

> Then Moses and the children of Israel sang this song to the LORD, and spoke, saying: "I will sing to the LORD, For He has triumphed gloriously!" (Ex. 15:1)

> When the Israelites defeated the Canaanites in Judges 5:3, they sang a song: "Hear, O kings! Give ear, O princes! I, even I, will sing to the LORD; I will sing praise to the LORD God of Israel."

> When David wanted to express a broken and contrite heart to the Lord, he did so through music in Psalm 51.

> In Psalm 108, David specifically says he will sing and make music with his soul, linking music and the expression of emotions.

> Psalm 147 says that we should express our thanksgiving through song.

And, of course, the Psalms are filled with commands to express our affection and praise to the Lord through music.

Ephesians 5:19 tells us to sing and make melody with our hearts to the Lord.

In Acts 16 when Paul and Silas were in prison and probably fearful for their lives, what did they do? They sang hymns to God.

James 5:13 says, "Is anyone among you suffering? Let him pray. Is anyone cheerful? Let him sing psalms."

And we will be singing as an expression of our affection for God for all eternity (Rev. 5:9ff)!

Scarcely is there a mention of music in the Bible without some connection to emotion. If anything is clear from the Bible's discussions of music, it is that God thinks music is important. So should we. Music provides a language for a right expression of emotion, and good music actually educates our emotions so that they develop to maturity. That is why those who say the purpose of music in the church is simply to teach or affirm truth are completely missing the function of music. Certainly church music can teach the mind, but if our only purpose is to teach truth, there are many far better ways to do so. Preaching, teaching, reciting doctrinal statements, for example, are better suited than poetry and music to express propositional truth. This confusion may be the reason churches view music with so much indifference. If our only goal is to teach and affirm truth through music, then to most people music seems to fail, and they are probably right. But music is not incidental; music is not just something nice we use to accompany truth. We should view music in the church as that which helps us express our affections and teach us what our affections should be.

Music as Expression of Emotion

As Christians consider truth and righteousness, they should respond with their affections. This is the essence of worship, both in a general, everyday sense and in a congregational worship setting. It is often difficult, however, to know exactly how to express those affections. This is especially true if we limit ourselves to expressing our affections with words only. As we saw earlier, words cannot adequately express what we feel. Church music—that is, poetry set to music—provides the language we need to express our affections. So in a church service, as we contemplate truth and goodness, we use music to help us take the next step and respond with our affections.

It is important again to acknowledge the interconnectedness of mind, will, and emotion. Emotion for its own sake is not the goal. Many contemporary churches have it right when they insist that expression of emotion is a critical part of the church's work. However, they often misunderstand emotion and, in the end, focus on emotion for its own sake apart from the necessary connection to biblical truth. Our emotions must be connected to biblical truth.

Other doctrinally centered churches have historically erred in the opposite direction, viewing the expression of emotion as somehow inferior to the intellect or morality. We must view emotion on the same level as truth and morality. Did not Christ say that the greatest commandment was expression of affection to God? But even here emotion is intricately connected to truth and goodness, for if we love God, we will keep

His commandments. So while we must move toward a better focus on our emotional maturity, we must be careful that our emotions are connected to biblical truth and moral goodness.

Music as Teacher of Emotion

No passage better illustrates this point of music as a teacher of the emotions than Colossians 3:16, "Let the word of Christ dwell in you richly in all wisdom, teaching and admonishing one another in psalms and hymns and spiritual songs, singing with grace in your hearts to the Lord."

Notice that Paul says we should teach and admonish each other with music.[1] I do not doubt that the teaching here involves using the words to teach truth and goodness as well. But I believe the primary part of man that is being taught by music is his emotions. This is evidenced by the phrase, "with grace [thankfulness] in your hearts," and in the parallel passage, Ephesians 5:19, "singing and making melody in your heart." Music helps us to obey the command in Ephesians 4 and to mature believers' emotions by actually teaching them. We can see this kind of teaching evidenced in Scripture. When Saul was in a terrible emotional state, David used music to change and mature his emotions (1 Sam. 16:23). When Paul and Silas were in prison, they used hymns to lift their spirits (Acts 16:25).

So that is why we use music in church. First, we use music to help us express right affection to the Lord. When we respond

---

[1] Some debate exists as to whether "psalms, hymns, and spiritual songs" qualify "teaching and admonishing." However, the grammatical structure favors this interpretation. See David F. Detwiler, "Church Music and Colossians 3:16," *Bibliotheca Sacra* 158, 631 (July 2001), 358. "To assign these datives to 'singing' would create an overload of qualifying statements and destroy the symmetry of the two participial clauses. Also to assign them to 'teaching and admonishing' is consistent with the unambiguous parallel of Ephesians 5:19 . . ."

to truth, music helps us respond with our affections when we might not otherwise have the right words to say. Second, good music educates our emotions, and tells us what we should be feeling. When we do not know what kind of affection we should have or when we actually have the wrong kinds of emotions, good music can teach us what kind of affection is right.

Implications

We can draw several very important implications from these truths about the purpose of music in the Christian's life and, more specifically, in the life of a church.

1. *Just as we should be striving to increase in our intellectual understanding of truth and our moral capacity for goodness, so should we be seeking to improve our emotional expressions to God.* We rightly make much of striving to grow doctrinally and in holiness, but we also need to make emotional development a priority as well. We should make it a priority for our children. It is a tragedy that music education has been largely removed from the schools. Music education used to be mandatory, because people realized that music helped develop the whole person—mind, will, and emotions. But our society has lost that vision. Therefore, it remains for the church to take up this responsibility and educate our families in music.

2. *Just as church leadership has the responsibility to teach the congregation in areas of truth and goodness, so it has the responsibility to teach them in areas concerning their emotions.* The pastoral leadership of a church makes de-

cisions regarding what kind of truth and what kind of holiness they will teach. But they also must make decisions concerning what kinds of emotions they will teach, and this has to do primarily with what music they choose. The congregation, then, should submit to the leadership's decisions regarding truth, goodness, and emotion and strive to grow in these areas. Another great tragedy that has occurred in our society is that we do not insist that pastors be musically trained. This has not always been the case. In fact, the great reformer Martin Luther said, "Neither should we ordain young men as preachers, unless they have been well exercised in music."[2] Luther was scornful of those who "want to be theologians when they cannot even sing." One of the biggest reasons church music in our society is shallow and debauched is that most, if not all, pastors are completely ignorant when it comes to music. We need to mandate music training in Bible college and seminary because pastors are just as responsible for the emotional maturity of their people as they are for their doctrinal and moral maturity.

3. *Just as not all emotion is appropriate for expression to God, so not all music is appropriate.* Not all forms of emotion are appropriate for expression to God. Our affections should be connected to truth, and they should be right and wholesome. We would never express love for our spouse in the same way we would express love for our dog. Likewise, we should never express love to

---

[2] Walter E. Buszin, "Luther on Music," *Musical Quarterly*, XXXII, 1 (Jan. 1946), reprint by Lutheran Society for Worship, Music and the Arts, 1958, 5.

God in the same way we would express love for our spouse. The same is true for many emotions, and each of us is responsible to think through what kinds of emotions are appropriate for God. And it is especially the responsibility of church leaders to make decisions about what emotions are appropriate for worship. Since music serves as an expression and incites emotion, it is, therefore, true as well that not all music is appropriate. We should use only that music that helps us express right emotions and teaches us to have greater affection for God.

4. *Singing in church is not optional.* Listening to preaching is not optional. Reciting doctrinal statements or reading Scripture is not optional. Being holy is not optional. Loving God is not optional. Neither is singing optional for believers. We should be concerned about our minds, wills, and emotions. Therefore, we should listen attentively to preaching and teaching, we should participate with eagerness when we read Scripture or recite doctrinal statements, and we should strive to educate our emotions through the music in church services. Our churches are filled with people who do not know how to rightly express affection to God because they refuse to participate in the music of the church. Someone who has doctrinal and moral maturity but no emotional maturity is an immature Christian. This is a great need in our churches.

5. *The music we consume outside the church is also important. It, too, shapes our emotions.* We've talked much about music in the church, but all music shapes our emo-

tions. That is why we must be concerned about what kind of music we listen to and perform at any time. If you have as your regular diet music that debases your affections, you are disobeying God's commands to mature your emotions. You must be very critical of the music you listen to. You should perform and listen only to music that actually aids your spiritual walk and matures your emotions. You should choose the best music that teaches you the kinds of emotions you should have as a mature believer. The main reason many people have difficulty with good music in churches today is they listen six days out of the week to debasing music. So, it's no wonder they cannot appreciate good music that expresses right emotion. Rock 'n' roll, jazz, and Country Western music contain debasing emotional expressions that Christians should avoid. On the other hand, legitimate folk and classical music can educate a person's affections and make them more mature.

God commands the church to establish mature believers. That means the church must aim at the whole of man—mind, will, and emotions. Therefore, our doctrine must be right, our teaching of holiness must be right, and our music must be right. Music is important to God; it should be important to His church as well.

For Discussion

1. What are various reasons you have heard for using music in church?

2. What is the primary purpose of the church?

3. Explain why words are inadequate to mature the emotions.

4. Discuss the two-fold purpose of sacred music.

5. Discuss the implications to this understanding of the primary purpose of sacred music.

CHAPTER TWELVE

Congregational Worship Music: God-Oriented

We have seen that worship is a biblical response to God resulting from an understanding of biblical truth about God. It is necessary, therefore, that to be used in congregational worship, music must be God-oriented. Yet much of congregational worship today is man-oriented. Services are designed for "seekers," with music chosen that will appeal to unbelievers and entice them to attend church services. Revivalism and the megachurch movement have shifted the focus of congregational worship from God to people.

But since congregational worship is specifically designed to respond to God because of truth about Him, God must be the center of the music used for that purpose. If our goal is God, then our focus must also be God. Music that focuses on man and his personal problems may be appropriate for other venues, but not for congregational worship. The music must express truth about God, and it must be directed to God.

Expressing Truth About God

Modern praise and worship music often expresses lots of praise without identifying who is being praised or why he is being praised. This is usually empty emotionalism, because true worship cannot occur without a reason for the response. Repetition of praise wedded with emotional music and void of concrete reasons for the praise produces shallow sentimentality. Telling people about your feelings does nothing; telling them the source of those feelings will give them a cause for the same responses.

Truth about God must be Bible-based. God is known in two ways: by His character and by His works. One or both of these should be present in congregational worship music as truth to which a believer can respond. The Bible is our only absolute source of truth about God. Therefore, scriptural truth about God should be the content of congregational worship music. There is more than enough truth about God in the Bible to fill 100 hymnbooks! Subjective truth about man or his problems is not appropriate for congregational worship, because it is truth about God that moves us to worshipful responses. Personal experiences or other subjective expressions of God are not as sure and true as biblical truth. Believers should be careful not to choose music with subjective content. Instead, the content should be about or to God.

Some often argue that subjective content is appropriate for congregational worship. First, they may appeal to the Psalms and insist that since many of the Psalms contain individualistic content, our congregational worship music may as well. That is faulty reasoning, however, because not every Psalm was intended for congregational worship. Scholars tell us that many of the Psalms served other functions.

[There are] royal psalms to honor the king (21, 45, 101), processional psalms (24, 95, 100), and penitential psalms for periods of national repentance (130). Other psalms (120-133), called "ascent" or "pilgrimage" psalms, may have been sung in connection with the annual pilgrimages to the Jerusalem temple. The Egyptian Hallel psalms (113-118) narrate God's saving acts for Israel and were sung in connection with the Passover observance, two psalms before, and four after, the meal.[1]

Special events at the court—such as the ascension of a new monarch, the enthronement of a new king or its anniversary, the king's marriage, his departure for war and his victorious return—undoubtedly called for special music (see the "royal psalms, " e.g., 20; 21; 45; 72; 89; 110). Other types of psalms, such as psalms of praise (e.g., 145, 147, 148, 150), psalms of petition (e.g., 44, 74, 79, 80, 83), psalms of thanksgiving (e.g., 30, 66, 116, 118, 126), and processional psalms (e.g., 24, 48, 95, 100) suggest the uses to which they were most probably put.[2]

In other words, the book of Psalms is a collection of Jewish poetry, some intended for congregational worship, but much intended for other functions of Jewish life. Because Israel was a theocracy their music was all sacred to a certain extent, but not all was intended for congregational worship. Isaac Watts insisted this very thing in the preface to his own psalter, *The Psalms of David Imitated.*

Though the Psalms of David are a Work of admirable and divine Composure, though they contain the noblest Sentiments of Piety, and breathe a most exalted Spirit of Devotion, yet when the best of Christians attempt to sing many of them in our common Translations, that Spirit of Devotion

---

[1] Hustad, 38.
[2] Carl Schalk, "Jewish Church Music History" in *Key Words in Church Music* (St. Louis: Concordia, 1978), 89.

vanishes and is lost, the Psalm dies upon their lips, and they feel scarce any thing of the holy Pleasure.

I come therefore to explain my own design, which is, to accommodate the book of Psalms to Christian Worship and in order to this, it is necessary to divest David and Asaph of every other character but that of a Psalmist and a saint and to make them always speak the common sense and language of a Christian.[3]

Therefore, we cannot say that just because some of the Psalms contain introspective, subjective material that our congregational worship music may also.

Another reason people will say that subjective, personal content is appropriate for congregational worship music is that believers must be able to express their individual, intimate worship to the Lord. Since every believer is different, there must be opportunity for each person to express his personal responses to the Lord. This will be addressed specifically in the next chapter.

This is not to deny that hymns of personal testimony are appropriate for congregational worship. However, there is a difference between a hymn that expresses a biblical truth that all believers enjoy personally (the care of God or freedom from sin, for instance) and a song about an individualistic experience. There is also a grand difference between a hymn of testimony that magnifies God and a song of experience that focuses on the experience itself. Good hymns of testimony that magnify God and focus on His works are certainly acceptable.

---

[3] Isaac Watts, *The Psalms of David Imitated in the Language of the New Testament, and Applied to the Christian State and Worship*, Online (http://www.ccel.org/cceh/archives/eee/wattspre.htm).

Truth about God in hymns must also be complete. Music used in congregational worship should be complete in its expressions of God's character and works. It should magnify God's attributes of greatness and goodness. Those attributes associated with His greatness are His self-existence (Ex. 3:14; John 5:26), infinity (1 Kings 8:27; Gen. 21:33; Ps. 147:5), perfection (Ps. 18:30; Matt. 5:48), omnipotence (Job 42:2; Matt. 19:26, Rev. 19:6), omniscience (Ps. 139:1-4; 1 John 3:20), omnipresence (Ps. 139:7-12; Jer. 23:23-24), immutability (Mal. 3:6; James 1:17), wisdom (Rom. 11:33; 16:27), eternality (Gen. 21:33; Ps. 90:1-2), and incomprehensibility (Ps. 145:3; Rom. 11:33). Those identified with His goodness are His holiness (Lev. 11:44-45; Ps. 99:4-9; 1 Peter 1:15-16), truth (Ps. 31:5; John 3:33; 1 Thess. 1:9), love (1 John 4.8), righteousness (Gen. 18:25; Deut. 32:4; Ps. 145:17), faithfulness (Lam. 3:23; Ps. 36:5), mercy (2 Cor. 1:3; Eph. 2:4), and grace (Eph. 1:7; 1 Peter 5:10). In choosing music for congregational worship, we should strive to present God as He is revealed in His Word.

Often modern praise music will focus exclusively on God's attributes of goodness to the neglect of His attributes of greatness. Believers must be sure that the music they choose for congregational worship magnifies the entirety of God's character and works.

Furthermore, the music style should be worthy of the truth. Since it is truth about God that is being expressed in congregational worship music, we must be very careful that the music portrays Him correctly. We do not want to portray God as romantic, shallow, or sentimental. Yet much music intended for congregational worship communicates those feelings. I will address this subject more fully in chapters 14 and 16.

It does not take a knowledgeable musician to understand that certain styles of music are more suited to particular texts. Even within the realm of what is acceptable and good, certain styles simply cannot support a given message. Some tunes are simple and light and do not fit a deep, weighty theme. Other tunes express certain majesty and should not be wedded with lighter texts.[4] Other music is passionate or sentimental and would not serve to portray God as He is revealed in His Word.

Directed Toward God

If God is to be worshiped, music used for that purpose must be directed toward Him. In congregational worship, if a song's purpose is to respond to truth, it should be directed toward God. A response toward others may often be appropriate, but in congregational worship, the response should be specifically to God. Believers must be careful that the music they use for congregational worship does not draw the "worship" to itself. Much modern worship music is so emotional that people get swept up in the music instead of focusing on God. Soon people begin to actually worship the music itself. Performers must also be careful not to draw attention or worship to themselves through flashy or virtuosic performing. Congregational music needs to sit on the knife-edge between distracting shoddiness and distracting flashiness.

The New Testament Church is not bound by the same rigid restrictions for worship that regulated Old Testament

---

[4] Many hymnologists have written on this topic, some delineating specific metric rhythms and melodic patterns that more adequately portray certain messages. For further study, see Lovelace, *Anatomy of Hymnody* and John Wilson, "Looking at Hymn Tunes: the Objective Factors" in Carlton Young, *Duty & Delight: Routley Remembered* (Carol Stream, Ill.: Hope, 1985).

Jewish worship. Yet that does not imply that those regulations were unimportant or have no bearing upon the Church today. God delivered such laws to His people to teach them timeless principles about how He wants to be worshiped. He wants our best. He wants only what is pure and clean. He wants work and preparation to go into what we present to Him.

None of our offerings to God earns merit with Him any more than spotless offerings in the Old Testament earned favor. Our goal in offering acceptable sacrifices to the Lord is not that we will somehow be more accepted. We are accepted only through the sacrifice of Christ on our behalf, and nothing we do changes our judicial standing before God. Furthermore, we must recognize that any "pure" offering we bring before the Lord will always be tainted by remaining depravity. Yet this is not different from "pure" offerings in the Old Testament. No animal sacrificed on an altar was perfectly spotless, yet God demanded that the best be offered.

The same is true with what we offer to God. Our sacrifices of praise do not earn us anything; we are already accepted in Christ. And our sacrifices will never be perfectly clean and spotless. But God deserves our best. If we are attempting to worship Him through our music, then we should be certain to strive for excellence in congregational worship music. That means that shoddy, shallow, poorly written music should be avoided, and only what is quality, well written music is worthy of an offering to God. It also means that those involved in worship music ministry should strive to do their best and be willing to sacrifice time and effort in preparing their music.

That should be obvious, but people are often defensive of music that is lower in quality. Many insist that since people are different and preferences are different, there are no demonstrable aesthetic standards by which we can and should evaluate music. For instance, Steve Miller, a defender of such musical relativism, writes, "Truly good music must be judged within a form by those who appreciate the form, not by those from without who neither understand nor enjoy the style."[5]

In other words, only those who like a particular style of music can evaluate its worth. This is faulty reasoning for several reasons. First, it fails to affirm the total depravity of man and the possibility that the effects of sin may mar tastes. Man is completely sinful, and even believers are not free from the stain of sin. Therefore, man's tastes cannot be the primary determiner of what is good.

Second, as we have already noted, though the Bible does not deal with the subject of aesthetics in a systematic fashion,[6] when we examine the whole counsel of God, we can observe principles that will help us determine what is good. As John Makujina says,

> Divine attributes such as righteousness, love, holiness, purity, majesty, order, reason, harmony, balance, and goodness should govern our evaluation and production of music. It is undeniable that variety and creativity are characteristics of God; yet whatever variety and creativity we exercise in the arts, our workmanship must reflect divine qualities if it is to glorify God.[7]

---

[5] Steve Miller, *The Contemporary Christian Music Debate* (Wheaton: Tyndale, 1993), 55.

[6] It should be noted that few major biblical doctrines are dealt with systematically in Scripture. We come to doctrinal conclusions when we correlate truth from various passages in Scripture.

[7] John Makujina, *Measuring the Music: Another Look at the Contemporary Christian Music Debate*, Second Edition (Willow Street, Pa.: 2002), 155.

In fact, the Bible commands us to worship Him in accordance with His perfections and beauty. Consider the following passages:

> Give to the Lord the glory due His name; Bring an offering, and come before Him. Oh, worship the Lord in the beauty of holiness! (1 Chron. 16:29).

> I will praise the Lord according to His righteousness, And will sing praise to the name of the Lord Most High (Ps. 7:17).

> One thing I have desired of the Lord, That will I seek: That I may dwell in the house of the Lord All the days of my life, To behold the beauty of the Lord, And to inquire in His temple (Ps. 27:4).

> Give unto the Lord the glory due to His name; Worship the Lord in the beauty of holiness (Ps. 29:2).

> So the King will greatly desire your beauty; Because He is your Lord, worship Him (Ps. 45:11).

> Out of Zion, the perfection of beauty, God will shine forth (Ps. 50:2).

> Yes, they shall sing of the ways of the Lord, For great is the glory of the Lord (Ps. 138:5).

> In that day the Lord of hosts will be For a crown of glory and a diadem of beauty To the remnant of His people (Isa. 28:5).

Aesthetic standards are observable, and we should strive to choose music for congregational worship that is good in quality. That does not mean the music has to be complex and impressive. On the contrary, music that is too challenging and flashy can do more to distract from excellent worship than to aid it. However, there is a vast difference between simple, well-written music (both in text and tune) and music that is shallow, trite, and poorly written.

Martin Luther is a perfect example of a theologian who demanded that worship music be aesthetically excellent. Luther's belief that music could educate the emotions and enrich the soul—that it could make better people—informed his aesthetics. Luther believed that kind of impact could be accomplished only through music with intrinsically good qualities. Blume notes that Luther "demanded that the 'musica artificialis' [composed music as opposed to music of nature] of 'fine musicians' and 'learned people' be used for the worship service."[8] He insisted that the church use only the finest music because he knew that only music composed with artistic excellence had the potential to accomplish his goals. His acclamation of the composer Josquin provides the perfect illustration of such aesthetic consideration. Hoelty-Nickel notes that Luther's observations of Josquin's music reflect the writings of Henricus Glareanus, who was a contemporary of Luther and used Josquin's music as a test case for his theories. According to Hoelty-Nickel, Glareanus taught that

> a work of art requires two prerequisites: *ars* and *ingenium*.
> *Ars* he interprets as the laws and rules of music that can
> be taught and learned. *Ingenium* to him means the original

---

[8] Blume, 13.

182

and creative impulse of the musician, which is purely a gift. Where *ars* and *ingenium* meet in the process of composing, there will necessarily ensue a perfect work of art.[9]

Hoelty-Nickel argues that Luther's comments about his favorite composer Josquin being "a master of the notes" reflect Glareanus's discussions of "art and genius."[10] Another example of Luther's insistence upon objectively good art being used for church music involves his critique of the music of Lukas Edemberger. Luther remarked, "He has enough of art and skill, but is lacking in warmth."[11] Luther insisted that "if anyone wishes to compose German hymns, let no one presume to do this unless he is endowed with grace for it."[12]

Principles found in section 2 certainly apply here as well. Too often believers have been satisfied with presenting to God mediocre music, whether in style or preparation. God is worthy of our very best.

Horizontal Effects

Although our discussion has focused on the argument that congregational worship music must center primarily on God, I do not want to imply that the worshiper will receive no benefit himself. Certainly, God-oriented music will edify and strengthen believers as they understand biblical truth and respond to it.

Some might insist that we should not be concerned only with the "vertical" in our worship. They argue that we also

---

[9] George W. Forell, et al, *Luther and Culture* (Decorah, Iowa: Luther College, 1960), 149-150.
[10] Ibid.
[11] Buszin, 89.
[12] Lehmann, 300.

need music and activities within our worship services that are horizontal for believers to be edified. However, it is biblical truth about God that will edify believers the most, not subjective truth about themselves. In addition, the most uplifting and beneficial activity a believer can participate in is the worship of God.

Over the centuries, man-centered theology has led men to organize services in such a way that unbelievers would be comfortable and more easily moved toward conversion. In each case, the music of popular culture was adopted to facilitate that goal. Charles Finney did it in the 19th century, and church marketing experts are doing it today.

That practice is faulty and dangerous, however, for two reasons. First, it fails to trust in the sovereignty and power of God in salvation. Men use human means and sinful methods to reach the lost instead of trusting God to do the work. The second reason is that such a practice results in neglecting congregational worship. Evangelism is certainly necessary, but not at the expense of congregational worship. We must set aside dedicated times for congregational worship as well as times for evangelism.

True worship, however, will be evangelistic. As believers magnify and exalt their Lord, unbelievers will witness the power of God. As biblical truth is presented, unbelievers will be confronted with it. Paul speaks of this in 1 Corinthians 14:25. He says if believers are worshiping God correctly, visiting unbelievers will likely witness the power of God and be converted. "And thus the secrets of [the unbeliever's] heart are revealed; and so, falling down on his face, he will worship God and report that God is truly among you."

Conclusion

The church has many functions such as fellowship, evangelism, discipleship, and worship. It is important that all of them are pursued. However, worship often takes a back seat to these other functions. Or, a church's worship often includes more horizontal activities than vertical ones. It is important that local churches set aside specific times for congregational worship, and that the music they use for such occasions be God-oriented. Sacred music that is more man-centered has its place in fellowship, discipleship, and evangelism, but not during the congregational worship of God's people.

For Discussion

1. Discuss the importance of expressing truth about God in congregational worship.

2. Explain that not all of the Psalms are examples of what should comprise the content of congregational worship.

3. Discuss the appropriate characteristics of songs of personal testimony in congregational worship.

4. Discuss how some sacred music might draw attention away from worshiping God.

5. Explain why believers should offer their best to God in their worship.

CHAPTER THIRTEEN

Congregational Worship Music: Doctrine-Oriented

Because we can respond appropriately only when we acknowledge biblical truth, music used in congregational worship should be filled with such doctrinal truth. Music that is trite and shallow may be fun to sing, but it is not appropriate for congregational worship. That is a time when believers are given opportunity to understand and acknowledge sound doctrine.

Shallow Truth and Congregational Worship Music

Often proponents of modern worship music defend its shallowness by saying it allows believers more time to meditate on one particular truth at a time. They complain that traditional hymnody is too deep with truth to be of lasting value to believers. Commenting on Charles Wesley's "Arise, My Soul, Arise," John Frame says, "Although it is a good teaching hymn, it is not easily remembered. I have sung it a hundred times or so, and I still have to open the hymnal to get the words right."[1]

---

[1] John M. Frame, *Contemporary Worship Music: A Biblical Defense* (Phillipsburg, N.J.: P & R, 1997), 103.

Instead, he praises modern worship music (which he calls "Contemporary Worship Music" (CWM) for its brief truth repeated over and over, maintaining that it allows believers to meditate on one truth at a time.

> A good CWM song in the same doctrinal area typically would focus on *one* of the fifteen points, surround it with hallelujahs, show how that point should matter to the singers, set it to a memorable tune, and give people some time to meditate on the wonder of that biblical teaching (emphasis original).[2]

Defenders of music with little content also appeal to the Psalms, arguing that many of the Psalms resemble modern praise choruses. We have already demonstrated that many of the Psalms were never intended for congregational worship,[3] but even if they were, an honest look at the content of most Psalms will reveal that they are nothing like modern praise choruses. Peter Masters argues, "All psalms (except five) contain sufficient matter to be converted into paraphrases or hymns of at least five hymn-stanzas in short or common meter. Most psalms are *much* longer than this" (emphasis original).[4]

It is also interesting to note that believers for hundreds of years have benefited from rich hymnody without the use of modern praise choruses. Instead, these people contemplated deep, doctrinal truth as they worshiped. In fact, these kinds of hymns had great evangelistic value as well. The hymns that George Whitefield used and promoted during the Great Awakening were the profound texts of Isaac Watts.[5]

Shallow songs with incessant repetition do not promote deep meditation and contemplation; they promote shallowness and

---

[2] Ibid., 103.
[3] See chapter 12.
[4] Peter Masters, *Worship in the Melting Pot* (London: Wakeman, 2002), 53.
[5] Arthur P. Davis, *Isaac Watts* (London: Independent Press, 1943), 207.

emotionalism. An honest look at the origins of modern praise choruses will show that they arose out of charismatic theology. Frame admits the ties between repetition and charismaticism.

> There is a tradition in charismatic circles to sing a short song over and over again, for perhaps ten or twenty minutes. I once attended a conference for worship leaders in which we sang, "I Love You, Lord" over and over again for maybe twenty minutes. It was an unforgettable experience.[6]

Donald Hustad also points out the charismatic emphasis of such songs:

> Finally, in the charismatic experience, all the exciting, extravagant, repeated songs of pure praise give way to a hush of awe, and, in silence or quiet song, believers may enter the very presence of God, the Holy of Holies, where (according to their definition) *worship* finally takes place. In this most intimate experience of relationship with God, believers may express their adoration however the Spirit leads, praying or singing in corporate tongues ("Spirit-singing"), in prophecy, or otherwise (emphasis original).[7]

If a church's purpose is to stir up the passions and create an ecstatic experience, repetitious praise choruses are perfect. If a church's purpose is to worship the Lord in spirit and truth while edifying and strengthening its people, praise choruses are inadequate.

There is a reason traditional hymnody has endured over the centuries and modern worship music changes with the wind. Even Frame admits, "The CWM movement greatly needs songwriters who will produce more thoughtful texts and excellent

---

[6] Frame, *Worship Music*, 121.
[7] Hustad, 289.

music"[8] and, "CWM needs greater doctrinal coverage."[9] The very nature of the genre prohibits such doctrinal depth. Shallow music cannot support deep texts.

Music of the People

Often people excuse shallow music (or preaching) by saying that new Christians cannot handle deep doctrinal truth. John Frame praises modern music on the basis that it is accessible to young or immature believers. "CWM is Christian music that is immediately accessible — to the young as well as the old, to the immature as well as the mature."[10]

This argument, however, does not hold up when you consider that the Epistles, written primarily to new believers, are packed with deep doctrinal truth. Paul's marvelous treatise on the doctrine of salvation in the book of Romans contains substantial truths such as predestination, election, justification, atonement, adoption, reconciliation, propitiation, depravity, justification, and sanctification among many others. New believers in Ephesus received a letter from Paul that addressed topics such as predestination, election, regeneration, adoption, depravity, and the doctrine of the church. Paul addressed the weighty topic of eschatology in his letters to the new believers in Thessalonica.

Remember, none of the believers in these churches, including the pastors, were seasoned believers. Many were probably mature believers, but this was not because of the length of their salvation. It was because these new Christians fervently studied rich truths.

---

[8] Frame, *Worship Music*, 126.
[9] Ibid.
[10] Ibid., 93.

Consider also the hymn texts that are found in Scripture and were sung by early Christians. Many sections of the New Testament were written in the patterns of classical Greek poetry and were quickly adopted as hymns in the early church. Here are some examples:

Philippians 2:6-11 (KJV)
Who, being in the form of God,
thought it not robbery to be equal with God:
But made himself of no reputation,
and took upon him the form of a servant,
and was made in the likeness of men:
And being found in fashion as a man,
he humbled himself,
and became obedient unto death,
even the death of the cross.
Wherefore God also hath highly exalted him,
and given him a name which is above every name:
That at the name of Jesus every knee should bow,
of things in heaven,
and things in earth,
and things under the earth;
And that every tongue should confess that Jesus Christ
is Lord, to the glory of God the Father.

1 Timothy 3:16 (KJV)
And without controversy great is the mystery of godliness:
God was manifest in the flesh,
justified in the Spirit,
seen of angels,
preached unto the Gentiles,

believed on in the world,
  received up into glory.

2 Timothy 2:11-13 (KJV)
 For if we be dead with him,
  we shall also live with him:
 If we suffer,
  we shall also reign with him:
 if we deny him,
  he also will deny us:
 If we believe not,
  yet he abideth faithful:
 he cannot deny himself.

Other passages considered hymns or portions of hymns are John 1:1-18, Ephesians 1:1-11 and 2:14-16, Colossians 1:15-20, and Hebrews 1:3.[11] These hymns sung by new Christians in the early church are certainly more substantial than modern praise choruses.

Modern worship is not the only music guilty of shallowness, however. Some of what might be considered, "good old hymns" fail the same evaluation applied to modern music. Note the following critique:

> [This style of music] is nothing if not emotional. It takes a simple phrase and repeats it over and over again. There is no reasoning, nor are the lines made heavy with introspection. "Tell me the story simply, as to a little child." The feelings are touched; the stuffiest of us become children again.[12]

---

[11] Wesley W. Isenberg, "New Testament Hymnody" in Schalk, 184.
[12] Spencer Curwen, *Studies in Worship Music* (1885) quoted in Eric Routley, *The Music of Christian Hymns* (Chicago: G.I.A. Publications, 1981), 137.

That sounds like it could be a critique of modern worship music, but it is actually a 19th century pastor describing the "American Gospel Hymn." Respected hymnologist Eric Routley characterizes this genre:

> The musical content of these songs is, in their primitive form, designedly slight. ...It is easier to find a description than a definition of the "Gospel Song," but apart from this extreme musical simplicity, what is common to them all is that they are songs designed to produce an immediate effect on listeners or singers; as solos they are sung *to* a listening congregation, carrying their message of conversion and salvation direct to their emotions through their evocative music: as community songs they are usually solos providing for an immediate congregational response in the refrain. Balancing the preaching for which they are preparation, they are themselves a form of preaching, with a minimal rational and maximal emotional content (emphasis original).[13]

Donald Hustad traces the history of this movement:

> Throughout the 19th century, the majority of evangelical churchgoers, especially those living outside large cities, were preoccupied with the popular hymnody, which evolved from the campmeeting songs and the Appalachian spirituals. Typical examples first appeared in the 1840s as children's songs, providing materials for the new, lay-centered "Sunday schools." The same style of music appeared with somewhat more adult, vernacular texts 20 years later and came to be known as "gospel hymns" or

---

[13] Routley, 137.

"gospel songs." It is impossible to overestimate the influence of these simple experience songs written by theological and musical amateurs and the grip they had on the general public.[14]

Additionally, Carlton Young connects the gospel song with pop music. "If it is anything, the gospel song is functional, direct, enthusiastic, and abounding in musical generalization, the essence of popular music[15] of any generation. (In the best sense, if you have heard one, you have heard them all!)"[16]

We must be careful, in our critique of modern worship music, to be willing to apply our own arguments to what has often been considered "traditional" music.

Doctrinal Truth and Congregational Worship Music

In the history of hymns, it is interesting to note that most of the early hymns were written to oppose doctrinal heresy. For instance, in the 4th century men like Hilary of Poitiers and Ambrose of Milan wrote their hymns to battle Arianism.[17] For centuries, the purpose of hymnody was to express and teach deep biblical doctrine.

Someone may argue that all important doctrine has been successfully put to song, and, therefore, new hymns need not to be written. Even if this were true, it does not mean we should, therefore, replace those hymns with shallow texts. Nor does it mean we cannot continue to write new texts to

---

[14] Hustad, 455-456.
[15] Young is using "popular" in the technical sense equivalent to "pop," not as an adjective alone. See chapter 5.
[16] Carlton R. Young, "Gospel Song" in Schalk, 175.
[17] Arianism is a heresy that denies the deity of Christ and the Holy Spirit.

express these truths. It is not true, however, that there is no room for new hymn texts. Even a cursory examination of the table of contents in a typical systematic theology will reveal that many doctrines have never been set to music.[18] Additionally, as new heresies arise, new hymns will need to be written to combat these theological aberrances.[19] Remember, without an understanding of doctrinal truth, worship cannot take place.[20]

Conclusion

We should not be afraid of songs that contain deep, biblical truth. It may take more work to understand and appreciate what they are saying, but when we do understand that truth, our response to God will be even more deeply worshipful. We should be willing to engage our minds, striving to understand important truths about God expressed through the music.

---

[18] Some examples might include the inerrancy and infallibility of Scripture, illumination, the church, and the nature of the kingdom, among others.

[19] Current heresies include open theism, ecumenism, Keswick theology, and new perspective on Paul's theology of justification.

[20] A significant point to be made here involves instrumental music. If worshipers listen to instrumental music in a church service without knowledge of the text, worship cannot occur. See chapter 17 for several suggestions to remedy the problem.

For Discussion

1. Discuss why sacred music with depth is more appropriate for congregational worship than shallow songs.

2. Discuss the important balance between excellence and accessibility in congregational worship music.

3. Discuss some of the New Testament texts that were likely early church hymns as presented in this chapter.

4. Discuss some sacred songs that are considered "traditional" that, nevertheless, fail under the charge of shallowness.

5. Discuss some of the benefits of having sacred music with deep, rich doctrinal content.

CHAPTER FOURTEEN

Congregational Worship Music: Affection-Oriented

In chapter 4 we discussed the difference between passions (which are involuntary, immediate, and fleeting) and affections (which are volitional responses to acknowledged truth). Affections are deeper and more lasting because they involve the whole of man responding to truth.

Because the very nature of worship is spiritual response to truth, the music used should develop deep affections for God, not simply emotional passions. Those affections will result from the way the text is written as well as the composition of the music itself. If the text has no solid, concrete basis for the music and if the musical style communicates emotional, sentimental feelings, it is not appropriate for congregational worship.

Much of this has to do with the objectivity of the text (which we discussed in chapter 12) and the depth of the text (which we discussed in chapter 13). Shallow, trite, sentimental songs are immediately gratifying and, therefore, arouse shallow passions that are not necessarily worship. Someone may experience a sentimental, nostalgic feeling because of a certain song, but he must not mistake that feeling for worship. In reality, instead of taking pleasure in God, he is taking pleasure in the smarmy, warm feeling he has. Again, the essence of worship and music is the response of the spirit; my concern involves what *kind* of response is targeted—affections or passions. This theme will be explored more fully in chapter 16. But for now, let's consider what is perhaps the most subtly dangerous form of passion—sentimentalism.

Sentimental Texts

In addition to shallowness, sentimentalism in modern texts does not foster deep affections for God, but rather surface emotionalism. This is certainly appealing to modern people because it fits perfectly with the emphases of pop culture. Kenneth Myers makes just that point.

> Sentimentality is as rampant in the culture of evangelicalism as it is in popular culture outside the church. Perhaps this is one of the reasons evangelicalism adapted itself to popular culture so readily. The friendliness of it, its lack of ambiguity, its sense of familiarity, its celebrityism—add to these qualities sentimentalism, and one realizes how much the two cultures have in common. But sentimentality may be the most corrupting of these qualities.[1]

This movement toward sentimental hymnody is not a new occurrence. Eighteenth century Pietism encouraged the same emphases—personal experience and feelings. "The subjective religious thought that emerged during the Thirty Years' War developed during the seventeenth century and reached its culmination in Pietism in the latter part of the century. ...Pietism emphasized the importance of personal religious experience."[2]

---

[1] Kenneth A. Myers, *All God's Children and Blue Suede Shoes: Christians & Popular Culture* (Wheaton: Crossway, 1989) 84-85.

[2] William J. Reynolds, *A Survey of Christian Hymnody* (Carol Stream, Ill.: Hope, 1999), 24.

Pietism greatly influenced the hymnody of the time. For instance, one of the early leaders of the pietistic movement, August H. Francke stated, "The goal of worship—and hence worship music—is the upbuilding of the worshiper. In one way or another this anthropocentric [man-centered] goal was behind nearly the entire church musical enterprise connected with pietism and rationalism."[3]

Additionally,

Friedrich Schleiermacher (1768-1834), as a child of both the Enlightenment and Pietism, pointed out yet another facet: worship (music) designed to edify must be for every man, and therefore simple and radically popular. This, in turn, spawned a wave of amateurism, particularly among the pietists, who upheld the faith of the common man against the onslaught of the best of rationalism. ...Simplicity (frequently naiveté) was elevated to ideal.[4]

The same thing is happening today. Personal experience, emotionalism, and "simplicity" are encouraged, and that leads to sentimental texts.

Many modern Christians, wary of deep doctrine and influenced by mysticism and an emphasis on experience, mistake feelings of nostalgia and sentimentality for worship. Someone may be moved to tears when they hear a particular "good old hymn," but that is not necessarily worship. It may be a fond memory or a nostalgic connection to the song. Certain texts lend themselves to this more than others, especially those that emphasize personal experience or "intimate encounters" with God (usually Jesus). A perfect example of sentimental hymnody is "In the Garden."

---

[3] Mark Bangert, "Theology of Church Music, Pietism and Rationalism" in Schalk, 341.
[4] Ibid., 342.

I come to the garden alone,
While the dew is still on the roses;
And the voice I hear falling on my ear,
The Son of God discloses.
And He walks with me, and He talks with me,
And He tells me I am His own;
And the joy we share as we tarry there
None other has ever known.

He speaks, and the sound of His voice
Is so sweet the birds hush their singing;
And the melody that He gave to me
Within my heart is ringing.

I'd stay in the garden with Him
Though the night around me be falling;
But He bids me go—through the voice of woe,
His voice to me is calling.[5]

It is hard to distinguish the sentimentalism and almost romantic affection of this text from a common sentimental love song except for a few select phrases. Surely God would be pleased with a more biblical, truth-based expression of love for Him. It is important to note, as seen from such an example, that this is not only a charge against modern worship music, but any music that stirs up the passions with sentimental texts.

Sentimental Music

The music of congregational worship can also evidence sentimentalism and emotionalism. It leads to what Peter Masters

[5] C. Austin Miles.

calls, "ecstatic worship." "Ecstatic worship takes place when the object of the exercise is to achieve a warm, happy feeling, perhaps great excitement, and even a sense of God's presence through the earthly, physical aspects of worship such as music and movement."[6]

It does not take a trained musician to recognize music that is intended to stir the passions. It may not be wrong in and of itself, but it is certainly not appropriate for congregational worship. Such music inherently bypasses the intellect and runs straight for the passions. It is not deeply felt affection resulting from understanding biblical truth; it is emotionalism, pure and simple. As Masters points out, it is not worship. "Music cannot really move the soul. It only moves the emotions. Valid worship starts in the minds. If it bypasses the understanding, it is not true worship. If it is overwhelmed by physical things, such as the skillful and moving performance of orchestras, it is compromised and spoiled.[7]

We must be careful not to choose music that appeals primarily to the passions, no matter how beautiful or moving it is. In congregational worship, we should be moved by truth, not by the music itself. The musical style should support the truth, and the music can aid our responses of affection, but it should not control them.

Worshiping God or Emotions?

The order of what happens with music is important. Worship occurs when believers hear and understand truth while the music helps express the response. If a person is simply caught up with the spectacle of the music, he is not

---

[6] Masters, 23.

[7] Ibid., 25.

worshiping the Lord. Instead, he may actually be worshiping his emotions and/or the music itself.

Again, the problem is not with music that elicits emotional response. All music does that. The concern involves *how* certain musical forms elicit emotional responses and exactly *what kind* of responses they arouse. God-honoring congregational worship music will cause a believer to understand biblical truth, and aid him in his expression of deeply felt affections for God.

For Discussion

1. What elements in sacred music might affect its influence on either the affections or the passions?

2. Define and discuss sentimentalism.

3. Discuss some sacred songs that encourage sentimentalism.

4. Discuss some of the problems with sacred music that target the passions instead of the affections.

CHAPTER FIFTEEN

Congregational Worship Music: Congregation-Oriented

On one occasion, I attended a contemporary praise service on a Saturday night. In the midst of pounding rock music and emotional praise choruses, the worship leader encouraged attendees to have "a personal encounter with God." I saw people with their eyes closed, swaying to the music, completely oblivious to the other worshipers around them.

That kind of conduct is very common in modern services. Even churches that do not use contemporary music or encourage charismatic emotionalism propagate the idea that worship services are a time for individuals to encounter God. What these people have forgotten, however, is that congregational worship is not the time for believers to worship the Lord individually. It is the time for believers to worship corporately. That does not mean it is simply a large gathering of people who worship individually, but it is a gathering of believers who worship God together.

In chapter 10, I established a biblical definition of congregational worship: *Congregational worship is a unified chorus of spiritual responses toward God expressed publicly to God as a result of understanding biblical truth about God.* The fact that the worship is congregational implies that believers will join in a unified response toward God. There is certainly a time and place for individual worship. It is necessary. Without it, congregational worship cannot take place. Therefore, when believers gather to worship the Lord corporately, music used for this purpose should be congregational in nature.

Because the purpose of congregational worship is that believers join together as the body of Christ to express a unified response to God, music that is individualistic or personal does not have a place in congregational worship. That kind of music may be appropriate for one's individual enjoyment or worship, but not for the congregation as a whole. Certain songs may express experiences or promises that are not applicable to every believer. Music used in congregational worship, however, should be limited to songs that express substantive truth that applies to all Christians.

Congregational Texts

The use of pronouns in congregational music plays a large part in this emphasis. The frequent use of "I," "me," and "my" usually indicates a more individualistic song that may not be fitting for congregational worship. We must look beyond the pronouns, however. There are many songs that use singular personal pronouns that are, nevertheless, corporate in nature.[1]

We must, therefore, look at the content of the music and evaluate whether it expresses truth that is individual or congregational. Much sacred music is very introspective and personal. That is true for modern worship music as well as older

---

[1] It is interesting, however, that certain hymnbook editors still choose to change these singular pronouns to plural ones. For instance, in *Lutheran Worship*, "I Sing the Mighty Power of God" is changed to "We Sing the Mighty Power of God." (Words by Isaac Watts in *Divine and Moral Songs for Children*, 1715.)

gospel music. That kind of text is not appropriate for con-gregational worship. Instead, we should choose texts that are corporate in nature.

Congregational Music

This applies not only to the content of the text, but also to the style of music. Many styles of music are governed by cultural trends. Such styles are constantly changing and going in and out of use. We should use music styles that transcend cultures and backgrounds—quality music that has stood the test of time and culture. Music that is trendy or narrowly cultural is not accept-able. Only music that crosses the barriers of age, culture, and taste is a proper vehicle for congregational worship.

For Discussion

1. Explain why a church service is not time for a "personal encounter with God."

2. What are some ways the texts of sacred songs might en-courage individualism?

3. What are some ways the music of sacred songs might encourage individualism?

4. How can sacred music actually encourage community in congregational worship?

CHAPTER SIXTEEN

Making Sacred Musical Choices

I have frequently heard people say that certain music is inappropriate for worship because it is "too emotional." However, since worship is essentially inward, spiritual responses to truth (John 4), emotion is necessary! There cannot be such a thing as a hymn that is too emotional. On the contrary, as we saw in chapter 11, the primary purpose of sacred music is to help us express right affection for God. However, what these individuals probably mean is that only some responses of emotion are appropriate for expression to God, and, therefore, only some music is appropriate for congregational worship. This is a very important consideration as we evaluate sacred music.

Appropriate Responses

Some music communicates right responses to God, like those we noted in chapter 4. God is pleased when His people respond to truth about Him with appropriate, biblical, spiritual responses. To glorify God is to magnify God's unique excellence through our responses. When music elicits responses like these, it is likely appropriate for worship.

On the other hand, some music communicates messages that are inappropriate for believers in any situation. For instance, through accurately representing the movements and passions of the physical act of love through sound combinations, music can communicate physical union. Since this is an act reserved for the privacy of marriage, public representations of this are certainly unbiblical. Another example is chaos, which can be easily represented through music, and is certainly wrong for believers.

There are other messages that are acceptable in some situations, but are not appropriate in congregational worship or when they are mixed with something sacred. These emotions may be perfectly acceptable for the secular music a Christian enjoys—music about trees and love and family—but they are not appropriate for expression to our holy God. These unacceptable emotions are often slight distortions of emotions that are appropriate. In the following examples, both will be compared and contrasted.

Sentimentalism vs. Adoration

Adoration to the Lord is a response clearly commanded by Scripture and appropriate for congregational worship. Adoration means to love intensely and admire.

Adoration, however, is often confused with sentimentalism. Sentimentalism is false emotion that is out of proportion to a situation and not justified by it. It is usually drippy, mushy, schmaltzy, slushy kinds of feelings that have no basis in truth. Unfortunately, churches are filled with sentimentalism. So many people are moved to tears when they hear a song, not because of any particular truth, but because it makes them feel good or they have some kind of nostalgic connection to it. That is not true worship!

Joviality vs. Joy

Christians should always exhibit joy (Phil. 4:4-7). As justified sinners, we certainly have a lot to be joyful about. Joy is not a skippy, chipper, "Ra Ra Ra!" kind of cheerfulness. It is not slaps on the back, cracking jokes, sarcasm, or a goofy kind of silliness. It is not an escapist, try-to-ignore-the-reality-of-hardship kind of entertainment happiness. It is not sweaty palm, butterflies in the stomach, giddy feelings in the chest love and joy. It is deeply rooted, Christ-centered, serious joy in the midst of persecutions, trials, and hardships.

Our society is an escapist society. What I mean is that people do not want to recognize reality; we do not want to acknowledge that things are difficult. Instead, we have comedians and entertainment and pop music and drugs and alcohol and all sorts of things that take our minds off how hard life is. But how long does that escape last?

It is not just unbelievers who view joy that way. Christians, too, have an incorrect view of what biblical joy really is. Christians, too, want more jokes in the pulpit and more chipper people in church and more silliness and feelings of happiness, so we slap each other on the backs and tell jokes and be sarcastic, all in an attempt to try to forget suffering.

God does not want us to ignore suffering; He wants us to rejoice in suffering. Think about one of the most well-known commands in this regard. In Philippians 4:4 Paul says, "Rejoice in the Lord always. Again I will say, rejoice!" Do you know where Paul was when he wrote that? He was in prison. I dare say that Paul knew more suffering than most modern Americans. And he had a right view of biblical joy. I think he expresses it best in 2 Corinthians 6:4-10.

But in all things we commend ourselves as ministers of God: in much patience, in tribulations, in needs, in distresses, in stripes, in imprisonments, in tumults, in labors, in sleeplessness, in fastings; by purity, by knowledge, by longsuffering, by kindness, by the Holy Spirit, by sincere love, by the word of truth, by the power of God, by the armor of righteousness on the right hand and on the left, by honor and dishonor, by evil report and good report; as deceivers, and yet true; as unknown, and yet well known; as dying, and behold we live; as chastened, and yet not killed; as sorrowful, yet always rejoicing....

That's a picture of biblical joy. That's the kind of joy that should describe us—sorrowful, yet always rejoicing, acknowledging and accepting the hardships that God has given us to test our faith and rejoicing in them. And there is no greater example than Christ Himself, "Looking unto Jesus, the author and finisher of our faith, who for the joy that was set before Him endured the cross, despising the shame, and has sat down at the right hand of the throne of God" (Heb. 12:2). That is not a silly kind of joviality. It is serious joy.

So we must consider this issue with regard to our music. There are a lot of gospel songs and hymns that express the wrong, silly, chipper kind of happiness that is not true, serious joy. There are many tunes that are bouncy, chipper, silly songs that fit better in a circus than in the communication of God's truth. There's nothing wrong with bouncy, chipper, and silly; but that's not joy. I am certainly in favor of singing silly songs and being goofy in the right circumstances, but that's not biblical joy. Otherwise, believers who live under oppression and are never "silly" or "goofy" are not truly joyful. Do not confuse silliness and bounciness and feeling good with biblical joy. Biblical joy is not "oom-pa-pa" circus music or "I've got the joy, joy, joy, joy down in my heart." Biblical joy is like what the final stanza of the hymn, "'Tis the Christ" by Thomas Kelley expresses.

> Here we have a firm foundation,
> Here the refuge of the lost;
> Christ's the Rock of our salvation,
> His the name of which we boast.
> Lamb of God, for sinners wounded,
> Sacrifice to cancel guilt!
> None shall ever be confounded
> Who on Him their hope have built.[1]

Biblical joy is not light and chipper; it is inexpressible and glorious: "Though you have not seen him, you love him. Though you do not now see him, you believe in him and rejoice with joy that is inexpressible and filled with glory" (1 Peter 1:8 ESV).

Levity vs. Community

It is important for believers to exhibit biblical fellowship with one another in the body of Christ. It is even important and necessary for believers to have a sense of community or "togetherness" as they worship the Lord with a unified voice. But often, in order to encourage those kinds of responses, churches will stoop to levity in their services. That may take the form of incessant joke telling or even a "handshake chorus" to encourage fellowship. But that sort of baseless lightness of manner takes place at the expense of many more-biblical kinds of responses. That does not mean church leaders should try to stifle what one pastor calls "real life humor" that

---

[1] Thomas Kelly, *Hymns on Various Passages of Scripture*, 1804.

takes place in the course of a service. What it does mean is that they should not try to manufacture irreverent levity.

Romantic Affection vs. Reverent Love

While loving God with all our heart, soul, mind, and strength is the greatest command (Luke 10:27), it should never take the form of romantic affection. Too many songs intended for worship communicate more of what two lovers would share than the kind of reverent love that God desires.

Sadness vs. Sorrow

One important appropriate response of worship is sorrow (Ps. 51:17; 38:18; Eccl. 7:3). Contemplating our sinfulness, Christ's sufferings, and the plight of mankind should elicit a brokenness or grief. But that should not be confused with sadness. Never should Christians lose the joy that comes only from a relationship with Christ.

Familiarity vs. Paternity

While believers are children of God and have a Father/son relationship with Him through adoption, never should Christians be so "familiar" with Him that they slip into irreverence. Never in the Scriptures do we find believers interacting with God on a disrespectful, familiar level. Even David, who had a tender, close relationship with God, does not use the kind of vulgar language with God that many Christian songs do today. Certainly God is "Abba"—Father. But as Michael Barrett explains, Abba is not an irreverently familiar term for God.

Notwithstanding the phonetic simplicity of the word, it is not to be equated with the equally phonetically simple expressions "dada" or "daddy" that English-speaking children so easily utter as their first appellation for their earthy fathers. *Abba* is not a nickname; it is not a childish term of sentimentality or endearment. Rather, it is an honorific title that expresses the utmost reverence and respect due to any father — and infinitely more so when referring to the Heavenly Father. The Lord Himself asks, "If then I be a father [Hebrew *ab*], where is mine honour"? (Mal. 1:6). Although every child of God has the privilege of approaching God as his Father and so addressing Him, none has the right to address the Lord as "Dad" or "Daddy." It may be cute and endearing when a child refers to his father in those terms, but it would be the height of irreverence to use such language in addressing God. The fact that the term Abba is easy to say is irrelevant to its honorific significance.[2]

Somberness vs. Sobriety

God commands believers to be sober (1 Thess. 5:6; 1 Tim. 3:2; Titus 2:6; 1 Peter 1:13; 5:8). This directly contradicts many of the inappropriate responses we have already seen (joviality and levity, for example). However, sobriety is not somberness. Never should believers be gloomy, melancholy, or grave.

Triviality vs. Simplicity

Simplicity in worship is certainly praiseworthy. God is pleased when believers offer modest offerings to Him. But nothing is commendable in triviality. Triviality deals with what is superficial, insignificant, or of little substance. To make biblical truth trivial is to cheapen it and rob it of its significance.

---

[2] Michael P. V. Barrett, *Complete In Him: A Guide to Understanding and Enjoying the Gospel*, (Greenville, S.C.: Ambassador-Emerald Int'l, 2000), 183.

Virtuosity vs. Excellence

God demands excellence and skill in worship (Ps. 33:1-3). But to show off one's talents through a virtuosic or "flashy" performance draws attention to the performer and away from worship.

Appropriate Congregational Worship Music

How, then, should we evaluate sacred music to determine whether it is pleasing to the Lord? We must carefully analyze each layer of the music.

Consider the Textual Content

This is the most obvious step, but many churches fail even here. Unfortunately, some church leaders and members mindlessly sing through songs out of tradition, never stopping to evaluate what they are singing. We must, however, ask some important questions to evaluate our music.

Is the text doctrinally correct?

Do we really examine the texts we are singing? We need to be careful to examine the texts of hymns and songs to determine their doctrinal accuracy before we use them in our congregational worship!

Is the text appropriate for congregational worship?

We must carefully evaluate our sacred music to determine if the message of the text (both propositionally and effectively) is really appropriate for congregational worship. Many messages are not. If we have a proper understanding of who God is and what He expects from those who worship Him, we will reject messages of irreverence, sentimentality, levity, or banality. What does the text say about God? Does it give Him the weight He deserves, or are the sentiments expressed more applicable to a husband-wife relationship than to fellowship with God?

Is the text congregationally-oriented?

We must examine the kinds of messages being expressed through the text to determine whether they are predominantly individualistic and personal, or objective and congregational. Because the whole congregation is involved in worship, the music we use to encourage congregational worship should apply to the whole body.

Is the text understandable?

Writing hymn texts is a specialized skill. Not just any poem will work for congregational singing. One of the most important factors involved in evaluating hymns is whether the text is understandable when sung. This was one of the chief reasons that Isaac Watts began writing hymns. The congregational songs of his day were filled with long, drawn-out sentences that were hard to comprehend while singing. As he began writing hymns, Watts determined he would write hymns with short phrases that could be easily understood. Some wonderfully rich sacred poetry, for instance, would not be easily accessible as congregational song. Consider, for instance, this magnificently beautiful poem by George Herbert:

Immortal Love, author of this great frame,
    Sprung from that beauty which can never fade;
    How hath man parceled out thy glorious name,
And thrown it on that dust which thou hast made,

While mortal love doth all the title gain!
Which siding with invention, they together
Bear all the sway, possessing heart and brain,
(Thy workmanship) and give thee share in neither.

Wit fancies beauty, beauty raiseth wit:
The world is theirs; they two play out the game,
Thou standing by: and though thy glorious name
Wrought our deliverance from th' infernal pit,

Who sings thy praise? Only a scarf or glove
Doth warm our hands, and make them write of love.[3]

This is a beautiful, doctrinally accurate expression of biblical sentiment, but it would probably not work as a congregational song.

Another important factor with this issue is whether the grammar of the hymn is in the current vernacular or is too antiquated. There are many similarities in this respect between hymns and Bible translations. We use modern translations so we can understand the Scriptures in our current language. We may have to set aside a good translation in favor of another because its language is too archaic. The problem with hymns, however, is that though we have many good "KJV"-category hymns—hymns that have great content but are perhaps a bit antiquated, we do not have very many "NASB"- or "ESV"-type hymns. We have plenty of "Good News for Modern Man" kinds of songs—songs that contain biblical truth at one level, but whose form trivializes or even contradicts the message.

---

[3] George Herbert, *The Temple. Sacred Poems and Private Ejaculations*, ed. N. Ferrar (Cambridge: T. Buck and R. Daniel, 1633).

We need to examine our hymns to make sure they are understandable, and perhaps we will also find the need to be writing more "NASB" kinds of hymns, hymns that are quality in content, form, and modern grammar.

Consider the Textual Form.

At the same time, we must be careful not to concern ourselves with clarity to the neglect of poetic beauty that touches the affections. As we saw earlier, form is just as important as textual content in the communication of meaning. We must not evaluate only the textual content; we must also examine how that content is "packaged."

Consider the vocabulary.

Authors will sometimes use vocabulary that is cheap or trivial-sounding in their songs. Some of this depends on current culture. For instance, the word "awesome," though an appropriate word to describe God, may have somewhat more crude connotations in our current culture. We should choose hymns that use worthwhile vocabulary and reject those which use trite words.

Consider the grammar.

Many songs are simply poor grammatically. If God desires skill in our musical worship to Him (Ps. 33:1-3), then surely shoddy grammar is not acceptable for congregational worship.

Consider the structure.

Some hymns are "whiplash" hymns. They jump from one subject to another with no continuity. One of the marks of good hymns is that the content within stanzas and between stanzas forms some sort of progression of theme. Also, the skillful use of poetic devices in hymns helps aid in the understanding and memorability of a hymn. Conversely, hymns with weak structures should be rejected.

Consider the Associations.

As we discussed earlier, associations do not make something evil, but they are often an accurate indication of what the music means. For instance, why is it that certain styles are always used to portray romantic love, or sentimentalism, or chaos, or aggression, or physical love? The fact that those styles are commonly used that way does not make them portray these things, but it does give us a window into their likely intrinsic meaning.

If I hear an airplane in the sky, and the glare of the sun is preventing me from seeing exactly what shape the plane is, how could I discern what the shape is? By looking at its shadow. Now, does the shadow make the plane have that shape? No, the plane intrinsically bears the shape. But the shadow does give me a good indication of what the shape is. With music, associations are often shadows, giving us a fairly good idea of what the meaning is.

Consider the Intrinsic Meaning.

Discerning musical meaning does not require an advanced degree in musicology or an extensive knowledge of music theory. Consulting experts in these areas is always wise, just like we would consult experts in science to determine whether smoking is harmful to our bodies, or just like we would consult a linguist to interpret a letter written in a foreign language.

But the fact is that the nature of how music communicates makes it possible for anyone to discern the meaning. As we noted in chapter 6, musical meaning is fundamentally connected to human emotion and natural human responses.

What does the music sound like?

To discern what music means, we just have to ask, "What does this sound like?" Remember that music reflects the natural, detectable manifestations of primary emotions. Most researchers agree that the most basic emotions are joy, surprise, anger, disgust, sadness, and fear. Each has discernable physical indicators. Music can also reflect other universal physical motions through rhythmic combinations, motions like marching, falling, sensual movements, chaos, and physical union.

When evaluating music for its worth, we should not get much more specific than that. If we try to assign sounds to physical objects or what anthropologists call "higher emotions" like shame, grief, or trust, we leave the realm of what is universal. Those kinds of interpretations are individualistic. But what we can do is discern what the music is intrinsically communicating on a basic, universal level. Again, consulting experts is helpful and wise.

Is the general mood appropriate for congregational worship?

After we have determined what basic, universal meaning the music carries, we simply have to ask whether it is appropriate for the situation in which it will be used—in this case, congregational worship.

There are certain kinds of meaning that should always be rejected. Immoral meaning should be rejected. If the music communicates sensuality, lust, physical union, or unbridled anger, then no Christian should listen to it, let alone use it in worship.

Inappropriate meaning should also be rejected. There are other kinds of meaning that are not necessarily wrong, but are inappropriate for congregational worship. Examples of this music are "Beautiful Dreamer," "Daisy, Daisy," and "Let Me Call You Sweetheart." While this style of music is not inherently sinful and does not seem harmful by our desensitized perception, it does not have the capability of carrying the deep, doctrinal, God-centered texts that should comprise the content of worship. This style of music is sentimental and trivial at best. Another example would be romantic love. Music that intrinsically communicates such emotion would not be acceptable for worship.

Additional Considerations

In addition to evaluating meaning, discernment in hymnody requires some additional considerations.

Is it well written?

Because our congregational worship is God-oriented, we should strive to offer Him our best, which includes our musical choices. We should aim at including music in our services that is well-written in terms of melody, harmony, rhythm, and form. A trained musician can be very helpful in evaluating these elements.

Is the hymn singable?

The nature of congregational songs requires that hymns be singable. Singability is accomplished through various uses of poetic devices and an attention to the singing abilities of the congregation.

Is the hymn memorable?

Because relatively few people can read music well, most people sing hymns basically from memory. Hymns, therefore, should be capable of being easily memorized. Continuity of content along with certain poetic devices can aid in learning, as well as a tune that can be readily grasped and remembered and an attention to hymn structures that aid in memorization.

Conclusion

If we are going to please God with the music we use in our congregational worship, we must be more selective and careful with what we choose. We must carefully examine our music to determine if its meaning is pleasing to God. God is not pleased when we choose things that are shallow, trite, sentimental, or that express sentiments inappropriate for a relationship with Him. He wants us to choose music that communicates messages that fit our purposes for congregational worship.

For Discussion

1. Discuss the kinds of emotion that are appropriate for expression to God.

2. Discuss the kinds of emotion that are inappropriate for a Christian in any circumstance.

3. Discuss the kinds of emotion that are appropriate for a Christian in some circumstances, but never for expression to God.

4. Explain the differences between joy and joviality. How can each of these be expressed through music?

5. Discuss the multi-layer approach to evaluating sacred music as presented in this chapter.

CHAPTER SEVENTEEN

Preparation and Participation in the Worship Service

Unfortunately many church leaders put little or no thought into preparing for a worship service, and many church services encourage members to maintain a "spectator" mentality. Methodologies change. Congregational worship methodologies are not prescribed in Scripture, and it is not my intention to prescribe any here. My goal in earlier chapters has been simply to lay a biblical foundation and set down certain philosophical principles for congregational worship music. Here the goal is to encourage pastors, music directors, and other church leaders to purposefully think through how the worship service should be done based on that biblical foundation.

Though methodologies can certainly change over time, we are still responsible to give careful consideration to our methodologies of congregational worship and the theology and philosophies upon which they are based. Unfortunately, many pastors and church leaders do not consider what their worship services say about their theological and philosophical beliefs. They either put little thought into the service at all, or their methodology is completely inconsistent with their professed theology and philosophy.

I once attended a workshop that was supposed to help church leaders plan the order of their worship services. Instead of focusing on objective factors in these decisions or asking how the order would best facilitate biblical worship, the speaker's major determiner was how the order would appeal to the people. He passed out several service orders and then evaluated them based on what kind of effect they would have on members of the congregation. In reality, his method for formulating a methodology of congregational worship was rank pragmatism, which seems to be the determinant for many popular churches today.

We have established the theological and philosophical foundations for a biblical congregational worship methodology in the previous chapters. The purpose of this chapter is to develop some thoughts about how our methodologies of congregational worship can flow from that foundation. Again, I do not intend to prescribe any particular service order or way of doing things. I would simply like to stimulate thought to make sure that the way we lead congregational worship fits with what the Bible has to say about the subject.

Formulating a Methodology of Congregational Worship

We have seen that true worship has two essential elements: a presentation of truth and response to that truth. Both of these must be present in a worship service for biblical worship to take place. Every element in the service, therefore, should facilitate one or both of these.

Establishing Purpose

The church exists for many reasons, some of which are worship, evangelism, discipleship, fellowship, mutual assistance, and expansion. Local churches gather at various times during the week to accomplish these purposes. It is important, there-fore, that church leaders decide which purpose or purposes they intend to fulfill at a given meeting.

Some purposes fit better with others. For instance, fellow-ship and mutual assistance are both horizontal in nature and involve church members interacting with one another. Evange-lism goes hand-in-hand with expansion. Some purposes, by their very nature, work better when they are the exclusive focus.

Worship is one of these purposes. Because worship is in-herently vertical, other purposes that are more horizontal often hinder worship from happening. Does this mean that no hori-zontal activity will occur during worship? On the contrary, since congregational worship is intrinsically corporate, an awareness of others is important. However, a specific focus on fellowship during times of worship may draw people's attention away from God. Likewise, though discipleship certainly takes place during worship (especially during times when truth is presented), more in-depth discipleship can be accomplished when there is possibil-ity for feedback and interaction between teacher and student.

Therefore, church leaders should determine what specific purposes will be addressed in particular gatherings. For in-stance, Sunday School may be used primarily for discipleship. A church may have a designated fellowship time, and many churches reserve Sunday mornings for congregational worship. The Bible does not explicitly tell us when or how churches should fulfill their responsibilities. The important thing is that local churches take time to determine when and how they will fulfill those ministries.

Preparation for Congregational Worship

Our lives are often hectic, and church members frequently arrive at a church gathering at the last minute. They race their children to the nursery and quickly slip into their seats right as the service is beginning. Unfortunately, these people do not actually begin worshiping until well into the service. They are frazzled because of the morning's activities, and their minds are so distracted they cannot focus on God or His truth.

Church leaders should keep this in mind when they plan congregational worship services. They should plan a period of time when believers can simply calm their minds and prepare to worship the Lord. This could be as simple as dedicating the first five minutes of a service as a quiet time. It is not a mystical time when believers are "ushered into the presence of God," nor is it necessarily explicitly "spiritual." It is simply a time when church members can collect their thoughts, forget about the cares of this world, and prepare to worship. Providing tools to stimulate biblical meditation such as a suggested Scripture passage or a hymn may be helpful.

Some people may complain that this is too serious and stodgy and that it hinders friendship and fellowship. We certainly want fellowship to take place, and scheduling time for fellowship is important. But if the service is to be an effective time of congregational worship, church members must be allowed a peaceful time to prepare themselves for worship.

The Service of Worship

Congregational worship is a unified chorus of spiritual responses toward God expressed publicly to God as a result of understanding biblical truth about God. Therefore, every element in the service must fulfill this purpose. Remember, every element should facilitate congregational worship—presentation of truth, response to that truth, or both.

The Congregation as Participants

Every member of the congregation is responsible to worship the Lord during a worship service. A spectator mentality of people in the pews is easily developed but clearly anti-biblical. People should be engaged in worship at all times during the service. If there is a lag between "events," use that time for prayer and response to the Lord.

As a side note, church leaders should not be afraid of lag time or silence between events in a service. How many times, after the congregation has bowed for prayer, have they finished to observe an ensemble that has "magically" appeared during the prayer? This kind of irreverence during what is supposed to be a time of unified supplication to the Lord is done simply out of pragmatism and a fear of "dead time" as an individual or group gets into place. Congregations should be taught to use silence as a time to respond to the Lord.

Congregational singing is one of the most important aspects of a worship service. It is the one event where all members of the congregation can verbally worship the Lord together. Congregants should make good use of this time to understand the biblical truth expressed in the hymns and respond to the Lord with their affections.

Worship Leaders

The purpose of the music director, instrumentalists, choir, and other musicians is to lead in the worship of God. It is not their purpose to entertain or perform. Their purpose is to lead the rest of the congregation in worship. The congregation should participate with the worship leaders.

During an instrumental number, congregants should meditate on the words of the music and notice how the musical arrangement strengthens the message of the text. If you do not know the words, open your hymnbook and meditate on the text.

During vocal numbers, strive to worship along with the group or soloist by understanding truth and responding with them. The music will aid in the learning of truth and the expression of response. If the song teaches doctrine primarily, try to understand its implications and respond to the Lord accordingly. If it expresses a response primarily, try to join with the musicians in your heart.

Word from God

We should view preaching as the primary time when God speaks during the service. This is the time when believers are confronted with clear, biblical truth from God. Every attempt should be made to be sensitive to conviction from the Lord. Worship occurs only when you acknowledge truth and respond with change, affection, or consecration to God.

Since every believer is responsible to respond to biblical truth, pastors should provide a time for response after the Word of God is preached. Responding to truth is not the responsibility only of those who "feel convicted" or raise their hands in an invitation. All believers should respond in some way every time they are confronted with scriptural truth. Giving the congregation a few moments of silence at the end of the message could facilitate effective response time.

Does Order Matter?

There are no prescribed service orders in the New Testament. Unfortunately, however, this fact has led many churches to view their service order flippantly or simply pragmatically. Church leaders should put time into thinking through their order of service. An order of service should accomplish two goals. First, it should provide the opportunity for true worship to take place. Since worship is response to truth, the service should make it possible for that response to occur. Second, a service order should help the congregation to be actively involved and readily recognize what they are doing.

These goals could be accomplished a number of ways. One might be to group service elements that predominantly present truth separately from elements that predominantly offer response. Notice the following service order, for example:

Affirmation of Truth
  Hymn, "Holy, Holy, Holy"
  Vocal Solo, "I Know a Fount"
  Hymn, "God Moves In A Mysterious Way"
  Appropriate Scripture reading

Response to Truth
  Hymn, "Praise Ye the Lord"
  Brass Quintet, "I Sing the Mighty Power of God"
  Choir, "Crown Him With Many Crowns"
  Giving: "O Jesus, I Have Promised"
  Hymn, "It is Well With My Soul"

This order may help the congregation understand what they are doing and motivate them to participate actively. Using a bulletin or overhead projectors to indicate what a service element's function is may help as well.

"Special Music"

Conservative evangelicals levy weighty charges against contemporary worship styles. They charge that those who use such styles are more concerned with drawing attention to a performer than to true, biblical worship. Unfortunately, however, some of those who point out such offenses fail their own charges with their modern practice of "special music." These churches, while avoiding such offensive elements as drums and clapping, have musical events within their service traditionally termed "special music." These are usually solo or group events that have been scheduled ahead of time for a particular service. There is nothing inherently wrong with having prepared musical selections within a service. Unfortunately, though, this practice has sometimes become no less performance-oriented than that of more contemporary practices.

Conservative evangelicals who are concerned with true worship are quick to insist their music is not a performance. They claim their music does not draw attention to the musician, and they adamantly criticize those whose music does. But a careful look at their music practices will show they sometimes fail their own scrutiny.

An examination of the term "special music" itself sometimes suggests a featured event in the service. It is almost as if the congregational hymn singing and other events of the service are secondary. The *special* music is the highlighted event of the service. Again, this is not necessarily the case with all prepared musical selections, but it has become so in some churches.

Churches sometimes make this mentality even more prominent by how they order their services and select music. The congregation knows that certain *special music slots* are more prestigious than others. Those who perform for the offering or directly before the message stand more prominently than those more toward the beginning of the service. Musicians who are used to performing in the morning service are insulted when they are scheduled for the evening.

Additionally, clarity of truth and undistracting excellence are sacrificed for virtuosity and showmanship. The fault here lies on the part of worship music composers and arrangers along with performers who choose "showy" music. The musicians strive to demonstrate their great musical abilities, showing off their every skill and, ultimately, drawing all attention to themselves. Conversely, the congregation views those who play a simple melody as inferior compared to the virtuosity of others.

The faults for this kind of mentality lie not solely with the musicians. Many churches have special instrumental music with texts that are unfamiliar to the congregation (at least past the first stanza). When a church makes no provision for the congregation to follow along with the text of a hymn that is played, they encourage a spectator mentality. The congregation has no option for understanding and responding to truth if they cannot read the truth anywhere. This kind of mentality can often hinder biblical worship because worship is a response to truth. Worship cannot take place without a presentation and understanding of biblical truth.

As we have seen, Jesus made this clear in John 4, when He said that God looks for those who worship in spirit and truth. He was responding to the Samaritan woman's questions concerning the proper outward forms of worship. He insisted that worship was not intrinsically tied to outward forms, but instead it was a spiritual response to truth. Worship is a spiritual response to God as a result of understanding biblical truth about God. Both truth and response must be present for true, biblical worship to take place. Hymnody certainly facilitates worship since hymn texts teach biblical truth, and music is the language of emotion. Music without truth can certainly stir up emotion, but that emotion will be shallow and unfounded. Truth must be presented as well.

In congregational worship, therefore, it is important that every facet of the service enable the congregation to respond properly to biblical truth. That means that the order of service, the hymns chosen, the manner in which they are played or sung, and the overall perception given to the music by worship leaders must promote truth and proper response to that truth. If true worship is to take place, special music must focus the worshipers' attention to biblical truth. Musicians must do everything they can to promote biblical truth through their music instead of drawing attention to themselves and their skills. These musicians should view themselves as "solo worship leaders" who are responsible for directing the rest of the congregation in true, biblical worship.

It begins with the choosing of the music. A solo worship leader should choose music that is pregnant with sound doctrinal truth. Truth should be the first and primary criterion for musical selection. Religion and worship start in the mind and then flow to the heart. Musicians must choose music that reflects this philosophy. The leader should choose music that supports the message of the text. Many sacred musical selections are composed with no consideration of the text. The only consideration of the composer or arranger is musical interest and showmanship. Solo worship leaders, therefore, should choose music that reflects the truth of the text. They should avoid flashy runs and arpeggios that do not support the text and choose music through which biblical truth can shine freely. The leader should also choose music that he can play or sing with excellence. Often musicians will choose music that is too difficult for them in an attempt to impress the congregation. As they stumble through the piece, they create distraction from biblical truth. Solo worship leaders should never choose music with a skill level that is at their highest ability limit. They should choose something that is well within their abilities, something they can play or sing with undistracting excellence. The most effective presentations of truth through solo music are those that simply support the text of the hymn.

For the same reasons, the leader must avoid music that is flashy or draws attention away from the truth and to himself. Most sacred music that emphasizes the performer's skills leads the focus away from the truth of the text and to the performer himself. One wonders who is really being worshiped in those instances.

Again, the musicians are not the only ones with responsibility in these matters. If, during instrumental numbers, there is no way for the congregation to read and understand truth, then the church leaders are at fault as well. The church should provide the means for understanding the text during instrumental numbers. Announcing the hymn number prior to the piece or printing the text in a bulletin or on screens will help.

Since congregational singing is one of the most important means for joint, unified congregational worship, solo worship music should enforce congregational singing. Instead of choosing hymns that no one knows or that are not even included in their hymnbook, musicians should choose hymns that will either strengthen the congregation's knowledge of what they already know or introduce them to unfamiliar, quality hymns that are in their hymnbook.

Special music in a congregational worship service can be very helpful to biblical worship, but it should not be performance-oriented. It should facilitate true worship in spirit and truth. It should provide the congregation with ample opportunities to understand and respond to biblical truth. Maybe the term itself should be replaced. Perhaps a term such as "prepared worship music" or something similar would better describe these service events.

Offerings

Offerings are sometimes one of these "featured event" times, and rarely do people really consider what is happening. It may seem in some instances as if people "pay their dues" and then enjoy the show. This could be solved a number of ways. One might be to have an instrumentalist play a simple hymn of consecration straight from the hymnbook, letting the congregation know the hymn number ahead of time so they can meditate on God's blessings to them and how they should respond in worship with their giving. Even having the ushers wait until the second stanza would give the congregants time to consider these things before they are distracted with the passing of a plate. Whatever solution is utilized, people should understand that giving is one important spiritual response of worship that every believer should enjoy.

Conclusion

Methodologies are not inspired; they are derived from biblical theology and philosophy. Our goal should be that our theology drive our methodology. Personal preference or taste is not the primary criterion. Our methodology of congregational worship should come from our understanding of the Word of God.

It is important that church leaders put time and effort into preparing their services of congregational worship. They should do everything they can to facilitate true worship. It is also very important that every believer sees his responsibility to be an active participant in every moment of the congregational worship service.

For Discussion

1. Discuss the importance of intentionally planning every element of a congregational worship service.

2. What are some ways that church leaders could help their people adequately prepare for congregational worship?

3. Discuss ways to encourage every member of the congregation to participate in all of the service. What kinds of things might encourage a spectator mentality?

4. Discuss various ways an order of service might encourage or hinder true congregational worship.

5. Discuss how special music could often be improved to encourage true congregational worship.

Conclusion

I am the oldest of three children, and when I was younger I liked to boss my two younger sisters around. I thought I was a big shot since I was older and bigger than they were, and I thought I had the authority to tell them what to do because they were younger and smaller than I was.

What I soon found out, however, was that I was not at all worthy of their obedience. When I would try to force my will upon my sisters, they, of course, would report these actions to my parents, and then I very quickly discovered my true place in life. I found that I had no basis for bossing them around, and that my parents were indeed worthy of my obedience as demonstrated in their actions toward me.

There are many Christians today who have forgotten who is really worthy of honor and worship. Whether through their lifestyles or through what they bring into congregational worship, professing Christians act as if they are really the ones deserving attention.

There is only one being, however, who is truly worthy of any honor. Passages like Isaiah 6:1-4 and Revelation 4-5 make that abundantly clear as they give glimpses into heavenly worship. In both visions we see hundreds and thousands of angels surrounding the throne singing praises to the Lord, as well as many saints doing the same thing. We find their song of praise in verse 11 of Revelation 4, "Thou art worthy, O Lord, to receive glory and honour and power: for thou hast created all things, and for thy pleasure they are and were created" (KJV).

That statement reveals the purpose of God for His creation. God is worthy of our worship because He created all things for His own pleasure. Understanding that should fuel our worship, both individually and corporately.

God Created All Things.

The Bible says that in the beginning, God created all there is. He created every atom of every molecule of the most distant star. He created this planet and all that is in it. And God created man. Therefore, God has authority over all things by virtue of His power. God's creation of all things by simply speaking them into existence demonstrated His great power. That in and of itself gives God ultimate authority over all things.

That God is the creator also establishes His authority over all. Romans 9 clearly teaches that the pot has absolutely no right to question the authority of the Potter. He can do whatever he pleases with what He has created.

Listen to Isaiah 46:9-11.

"I am God, and there is none else; I am God, and there is none like me. Declaring the end from the beginning, and from ancient times the things that are not yet done, saying, My counsel shall stand, and I will do all my pleasure....I have spoken it, I will bring it to pass; I have purposed it, I will also do it" (KJV).

In Daniel 4 King Nebuchadnezzar takes credit for the wonders of his kingdom and then spends seven years crawling through the wilderness like a beast. At the end of the seven years he declares, "All the inhabitants of the earth are reputed as nothing: and he doeth according to his will in the army of heaven, and among the inhabitants of the earth: and none can stay his hand, or say unto him, What doest thou?" (v. 35 KJV).

Ephesians 1:11 says that God works all things after the counsel of His will. No one can question what the Lord does, because He created all things and, therefore, can do what He pleases. That is not like Pinocchio! God's creation cannot just defy its Creator and do what it wants.

The question, then, is what has God chosen to do with His creation? Why did God create all things? Was there something lacking in God that He had to create the universe? Absolutely not. Well then why did God create all things? Revelation 4:11 tells us that God created all things for His own pleasure.

God Created All Things for His Own Pleasure.

Everything in God's creation exists to bring Him pleasure. That is what it means to glorify Him. To glorify God is to accomplish God's purpose and bring Him pleasure. That is why 1 Corinthians 10:31 tells us to "do all to the glory of God," whether we eat or drink or whatever we do. That is why we were created. We can see that truth throughout Scripture.

The very purpose of our lives is to serve God's purposes. Acts 13:36 says that when David served his purpose in his generation according to the will of God, he died. God is our ultimate end and when we have finished our purpose according to His will, He will take us from this earth. Our good works find their end in God. Matthew 5:16, "Let your light shine before others, so that they may see your good works and give glory to your Father who is in heaven" (ESV). Even our ministry and service to men find their end in God. First Peter 4:11 says that men minister so "that in all things God may be glorified." Everything that we do in our lives, even our very existence is for the glory of God. God created all things for His pleasure.

That is the foundational truth in this whole discussion. The most important person in God's mind is Himself. He does all things for the sake of His own name. Let's take a quick survey of Scripture to see that truth.

Why did God create man? Was he lacking in anything? No. God was completely sufficient in Himself in eternity past. But in creating the universe, God decided to go public with His glory—to make the wonders of His character known.

Why did God choose Israel? Second Samuel 7:23, "And who is like Your people, like Israel, the one nation on the earth whom God went to redeem for Himself as a people, to make for Himself a name?"

Why did God raise Pharaoh up in Egypt? In Exodus 9:16 God, through Moses, says to Pharaoh, "But indeed for this purpose I have raised you up, that I may show My power in you, and that My name may be declared in all the earth."

Why did God harden Pharaoh's heart and send him merciless plagues and finally defeat him? In all those instances, God says it was so they would know that He was Lord.

Why did God save Israel? Psalm 106:8 says, "Nevertheless He saved them for His name's sake, That He might make His mighty power known."

Why did God send Christ to earth? Romans 15:9 reveals that it was "that the Gentiles might glorify God."

Jesus reveals His purpose for coming to earth in John

12:27-28, "But for this purpose I came to this hour. Father, glorify Your name."

In John 17:1 he says, "Father, the hour has come. Glorify Your Son, that Your Son also may glorify You." And in verse four, "I have glorified You on the earth. I have finished the work which You have given Me to do."

God rescued us from our sin so we might see and savor the glory of God.

Why did Christ receive us into His fellowship? Romans 15:7 says that it was for the glory of God.

Why does God forgive sins? Isaiah 43:25 says, "I, even I, am He who blots out your transgressions for My own sake; And I will not remember your sins."

Why has God delayed His wrath to punish rebellious sinners? Isaiah 48:9 says, "For My name's sake I will defer My anger, And for My praise I will restrain it from you, So that I do not cut you off."

Why is Christ coming again? Second Thessalonians 1:9-10 says, "These shall be punished with everlasting destruction from the presence of the Lord and from the glory of His power, when He comes, in that Day, to be glorified in His saints and to be admired among all those who believe, because our testimony among you was believed."

Why was the Scripture written? Psalm 102:18 says, "This will be written for the generation to come, That a people yet to be created may praise the LORD."

What is the ultimate end of God's eternal plan? Habakkuk 2:14 tells us clearly: "For the earth will be filled with the knowledge of the glory of the LORD, as the waters cover the sea."

From beginning to end, the driving impulse of God's heart is to be praised for His glory. From creation to consummation

His ultimate allegiance is to Himself. His unwavering purpose in all He does is to be marveled at for His grace and power. He is infinitely jealous for His reputation when He says, "For my own sake, for my own sake I do it...My Glory I will not give to another" (Isaiah 48:11 ESV). The great theologian Jonathan Edwards sums it up when he says, "The great end of God's works, which is so variously expressed in Scripture, is indeed but one; and this one end is most properly and comprehensively called the glory of God."[1]

So we see very clearly that all things were created for God's pleasure and that everything God does in this universe is for His glory and pleasure. So what, then, does this mean for you and me? What impact will these clear truths from Scripture have on each of us?

God is Worthy of our Worship because He Created All Things for His Own Pleasure.

Worship in its most basic general sense is living in such a way that we ascribe due glory to God. We do it by taking pleasure in Him over all other earthly pleasures. Since He created all things for His own pleasure, He expects all His creation to accomplish that purpose. Therefore, we understand that we were created to be worshipers of God, and we fulfill that purpose by living to glorify God. How is that accomplished?

Romans 3:23 says that all have sinned. How? By falling short of God's glory, failing to accomplish the purpose for which we were created. That is the very core of sin. All the good and righteous things a person accomplishes reflect that person's reason for being: to magnify the glory of God. To

---

[1] Jonathan Edwards, "The Dissertation Concerning the End," in Piper, *God's Passion*, 246.

magnify God's glory is like functioning as a telescope. A telescope sees something huge and magnificent but far away and brings it close and real. That is what we do when we magnify the glory of God. We bring the beauty and glory and majesty of the Lord right up close so people can see it. We do so by delighting in His beauty and glory and majesty.

That is the essence of worship. Worship magnifies the glory of the Lord. And that is the purpose of our very existence. It is why God redeemed us. Worship is at the heart of the gospel. We've seen that God does all things for His own glory and pleasure, and His saving people is no exception. Ephesians 1 clearly teaches that God is working in salvation for His good pleasure. God desires to call out a people for His name's sake. 1 John 2:12 says, "I write to you, little children, Because your sins are forgiven you for His name's sake." The ultimate purpose of salvation is to bring glory and pleasure to the Lord. In saving people, God creates worshipers for Himself.

Perhaps you have read through this entire book, but you are not yet a worshiper of God. You have not submitted to Him in saving faith and, therefore, are not doing what you have been created to do. The Bible clearly teaches that God is worthy of your worship! He created you for that purpose and makes it possible through the sacrifice of His Son. And the benefits of being a worshiper of the one true God are wonderful! Be assured, you will accomplish God's purpose for you one way or another. You can either surrender to God now and worship Him, or you will worship Him one day just before you are thrown into eternal punishment.

Worship is also at the heart of obedience to God. God's commands are not arbitrary. He didn't just sit down one day and decide to make up a list of rules. The commands for us in Scripture are rooted in the very character of God. His justice and holiness and splendor demand such things from His creation. Therefore, to disobey God's commands is an affront to the very character and glory of God. Because God's laws flow from His character, when we do something against those laws, we are acting against His character. God is worthy of our worship, and we should not do anything against the character and glory of God. On the flipside, when we obey God's commands, we magnify the glory of God, thereby worshiping Him. We should be constantly striving to follow the Lord's commands for our lives, because He is worthy of our worship. Romans 12:1-2 tells us that our reasonable service of worship is to not be conformed to the world but to be transformed by the renewing of our minds.

God Is Worthy Enough for Us to Consider Carefully How We Worship.

God deserves our worship because He created all things for His own pleasure. That means we should be willing to consider carefully *every* aspect of our worship, both in our lifestyle and in our congregational gatherings.

I am often amazed at individuals who are quite concerned about the form a preacher uses to deliver his message, but at the same time, are ambivalent regarding the form a piece of music uses to deliver its message. Not only are they concerned about the doctrinal content of a preacher's sermon, but they are also concerned about the way in which he presents it. They rightly understand that the manner in which truth is preached weighs heavily upon its impact and effect upon the listener. If a preacher fills his sermons with jokes and irreverent humor, the message—no matter how correct—will seem light and irreverent. But if a preacher proclaims the truth of God with authority and sobriety, that same truth will be received with reverence.

And yet, some of these same people who rightly concern themselves with preaching forms ignore musical forms. They insist that as long as a song's textual content is biblically accurate, it doesn't matter how it is presented.

But the same principles that apply to preaching apply to the way in which truth is sung. Both methods of presenting truth are important to the life of the Church, and with both presentations we must be concerned with form. In reality, sacred music is a form of preaching; it preaches to the heart through the head. And if our musical forms communicate irreverence or banality, the truth they present will have little spiritual impact.

God cares about congregational worship, and He cares about how He is worshiped. Much flexibility exists with the forms that we use or the structure of our services. But the theology and philosophy beneath any form or structure we use must be consistent. We must present biblical truth in such a way that people understand it and respond properly to it. That will take a lot of thought, consideration, and preparation, especially on the part of church leaders. But God will be pleased with our efforts. He is worthy of it. To Him be all glory.

For Discussion

1. How has your understanding of the purpose of congregational worship music changed as a result of this book?

2. Discuss some music you are currently using in congregational worship that might actually hinder true worship.

3. What, specifically, can you do to change your thinking and methodology concerning congregational worship?

4. What, specifically, can you change in your life to better magnify the glory of God?

A Plea to Teach Children Hymns

Evangelicals bemoan the fact that a "generation gap" exists between older and younger professing believers. But could it be that the older believers have actually created the problem?

Two problems exist: Children and teenagers do not care for solid hymns or long sermons, and modern young people's sacred music has been severely dumbed down. Which came first: the dislike of hymns or the dumbing down of sacred music (the chicken or the egg)? The answer to that question may not be so easy to determine, but it is clear that parents must provide the solution.

The first issue contributing to the problem is that parents (and adults in general) do not give children enough credit. For some reason, they assume that young people cannot handle deep, biblical truths or solid, doctrinally rich hymns. They have bought into the secular psychology that says, "Children will be children." In other words, do not expect too much out of young people. Adults seem to assume that children need silly, trivial music and activities to keep them occupied. Parents who defend their children's immaturity are actually encouraging the generation gap.

That leads to a second issue. Parents fuel the problem by exposing their children only to the trivial, light, and shallow. They assume children can handle nothing more than Bible stories and simple verses. They allow their children's music tastes to be shaped exclusively by trivial choruses and silly songs with slight truth. These same songs comprise the musical selections of Sunday Schools and other children's gatherings. It is no wonder children do not know good, historic hymnody. It is no wonder the same songs children grew up with are now being included in hymnbooks for adults. Young people, however, are very capable of understanding and appreciating deep truth. They can be trained to sit under lengthy teaching. They can be taught to enjoy good music. The problem is not lack of ability. The problem is lack of education.

There is certainly nothing inherently wrong with simple truth and enjoyable activities for children. But when children are not stretched—when they are not encouraged to expand their knowledge and preferences—how can they be expected to grow to maturity? From their child's earliest years, it should be the parents' goal for their children to grow out of the shallow and trivial. Yet parents actually encourage the opposite, encouraging their children to remain immature well into their young adult years—and beyond.

The solution is to expect more from children. Teach them deep truth and solid hymnody. Certainly, present the truth on their level, explain the content, and make sure they understand it. Use terms and illustrations they can readily identify. But hold high expectations, not low. Expect much, not little.

The church needs to take responsibility, too. Sunday School and other children's gatherings should not be times to encourage and promote silly songs or immaturity. Those gatherings are the perfect times to immerse the children in great hymnody, to teach them what good hymns mean and why they are good. The goal for children should be to train them to remain in the worship service, actively participating in what is going on. Using Sunday School to prepare them for what is coming will help them to participate more actively and to appreciate true worship.

Adults must stop catering to the immaturity in young people. If they want to bridge the so-called "generation gap," they need to expect more of children, train them to understand and appreciate deep truth and solid hymns, and help them grow to be mature by weaning them from trivial expressions of praise to God.

APPENDIX B

Classic Hymns Categorized by Doctrine

This list of hymns is not intended to be exhaustive, but rather a list of examples of classic, doctrinally rich hymns supported by ennobling tunes. The list was developed to accompany the excellent children's catechism program, Kids4Truth (www.clubs.kids4truth.com).

1. The Bible

Break Thou the Bread of Life | BREAD OF LIFE
By Grace I Am a Heir of Heav'n | NEUMARK
God, in the Gospel of His Son | GERMANY
Holy Bible, Book Divine | ALETTA
How Firm a Foundation | FOUNDATION
O Word of God Incarnate | MUNICH
Thy Word Is Like a Garden | FOREST GREEN

2. The Greatness of God

A Mighty Fortress Is Our God | EIN' FEST BURG
All Glory, Laud, and Honor | ST. THEODULPH
Holy, Holy, Holy | NICAEA

Immortal, Invisible, God Only Wise | ST DENIO
Mighty God, While Angels Bless Thee | HYMN TO JOY
O Worship the King | LYONS
Praise, My Soul, the King of Heaven | LAUDA ANIMA
Praise Ye the Lord | LOBE DEN HERREN
Rejoice, the Lord is King | DARWALL
Sing Praise to God Who Reigns Above | MIT FREUDEN ZART

3. The Goodness of God

All People That On Earth Do Dwell | OLD HUNDRETH
Great Is Thy Faithfulness | FAITHFULNESS
If Thou But Suffer God to Guide Thee | NEUMARK
Let Us, With a Gladsome Mind | MONKLAND
Now Thank We All Our God | NUN DANKET ALLE GOTT
O Praise the Lord, For He Is Good | GOSHEN
O Thou In Whose Presence | DAVIS
Savior, Like a Shepherd Lead Us | BRADBURY
Sun of My Soul | HURSLEY
The King of Love, My Shepherd Is | ST. COLUMBA
The Lord Has Heard and Answered Prayer | REST

4. The Trinity

All Glory Be To Thee, Most High | ALLEIN GOTT
Come Thou Almighty King | ITALIAN HYMN
Eternal Father, Strong To Save | MELITA
Holy, Holy, Holy | NICAEA
O Father, Thou Whose Love Profound | ROCKINGHAM
O Trinity, Most Blessed Light | BROMLEY
Praise God, From Whom All Blessings Flow | OLD HUNDRETH
Praise Ye the Triune God | FLEMMING
Thou, the God Who Changes Never | KIMBRO

5. Creation

All Creatures of Our God and King | LASST UNS ERFREUEN
All Things Bright and Beautiful | ROYAL OAK
From All That Dwell Below the Skies | DUKE STREET
God, Who Made The Earth | SOMMERLIED
I Sing the Mighty Power of God | ELLACOMBE
The Heav'ns Declare the Glory | UXBRIDGE
The Spacious Firmament on High | CREATION
This Is My Father's World | TERRA PATRIS

6. God's View of Man

Come Thou Fount of Every Blessing | NETTLETON
Come, Ye Sinners, Poor and Needy | RESTORATION
Father, I Know That All My Life | MORWELLHAM
From Depths of Woe | AUS TIEFER NOT
God, Be Merciful to Me | REDHEAD
How Sad Our State by Nature Is | SASHA
Mighty Mortal, Boasting Evil
O God, the Rock of Ages | GREENLAND
Teach Me the Measure of My Days | ST. FLAVIAN
The Foolish in Their Hearts Exclaim

7. God's Law

Blest Are the Undefiled in Heart | DOWNS
More Love To Thee | MORE LOVE TO THEE
Teach Me, O Lord, Thy Way of Truth | BISHOP
That Man is Blest Who, Fearing God | IRISH
The Law of God Is Good and Wise | ERHALT UNS, HERR
The Perfect Righteousness of God | MENDON
Thy Servant, Blessed By Thee, Shall Live | DUNDEE

8. Jesus Christ

All Hail the Power of Jesus' Name | CORONATION
Crown Him with Many Crowns | DIADEMATA
Fairest Lord Jesus | CRUSADERS' HYMN
How Sweet the Name of Jesus Sounds | ST. PETER
Jesus, Thou Joy of Loving Hearts | QUEBEC
Jesus, the Very Thought of Thee | ST. AGNES
My Jesus, I Love Thee | GORDON
Of the Father's Love Begotten | DIVINUM MYSTERIUM
Praise the Savior | ACCLAIM
The Name High Over All | HIGH OVER ALL
When Morning Gilds the Skies | LAUDEN DOMINI

9. The Gospel

Alas, and Did My Savior Bleed? | MARTYRDOM
And Can It Be? | SAGINA
Arise, My Soul, Arise | LENOX
Hallelujah, What a Savior | MAN OF SORROWS
Hark! The Voice of Love and Mercy | BRYN CALFARIA
Jesus, Thy Blood and Righteousness | GERMANY
My Faith Looks Up To Thee | OLIVET
My Song Is Love Unknown | ST JOHN
O Sacred Head Now Wounded | PASSION CHORALE
Stricken, Smitten, and Afflicted | O MEIN JESU, ICH
MUSS STERBEN
When I Survey the Wondrous Cross | HAMBURG

10. Sanctification

Am I a Solder of the Cross? | ARLINGTON
Be Thou My Vision | SLANE
I'm Not Ashamed | ARLINGTON

May the Mind of Christ My Savior | ST. LEONARDS
More Love to Thee | NEARER TO THEE
Nearer, Still Nearer | MORRIS
O For a Heart to Praise My God | AZMON
Soldiers of Christ, Arise | DIADEMATA
Take My Life | HENDON
Trust and Obey | TRUST AND OBEY

11. The Sovereignty of God

Be Still, My Soul | FINLANDIA
Forever Settled in the Heav'ns | DUKE STREET
God Moves in a Mysterious Way | DUNDEE
God the Lord is King | ARDUDWY
Hallelujah, Praise Jehovah | KIRKPATRICK
Hast Thou Not Known | DUNDEE
O God, Our Help in Ages Past | ST. ANNE
Savior, Like a Shepherd Lead Us | BRADBURY
Sing Praise to God Who Reigns Above | MIT FREUDEN ZART
Thou Sweet Beloved Will of God | GERMANY
Thy Way, Not Mine, O Lord | ST. CECILIA

12. Future Events

Behold the Glories of the Lamb | MARTYRDOM
Glorious Things of Thee Are Spoken | AUSTRIAN HYMN
Immanuel's Land | RUTHERFORD
Jerusalem the Golden | EWING
Jesus Shall Reign | DUKE STREET
Joy to the World | ANTIOCH
Lo! He Comes | CWM RHONDDA
O What Their Joy and Their Glory Must Be |
    O QUANTA QUALIA

A Guide to Building a Classical and Sacred Music Library

My intention behind this guide is two-fold: (1) To provide examples of what I believe to be music that rightly ennobles the affections. (2) To provide a starting place for someone who desires to replace his current listening repertory with music that will rightly ennoble his affections.

Favorite Classical Pieces

ALBINONI: Adagio for Strings and Organ
BACH: Brandenburg Concertos
BACH: Cantata No. 80
BACH: Concerto for Two Violins
BACH: Suites for Orchestra
BACH: Suites for Cello
BARBER: Adagio for Strings
BARTOK: Concerto for Orchestra
BEETHOVEN: Piano Concerto No. 5 "Emperor"
BEETHOVEN: Violin Concerto in D
BEETHOVEN: Piano Sonata No. 14 "Moonlight"
BEETHOVEN: Piano Trio No. 6 "Archduke"
BEETHOVEN: Symphony No. 3 "Eroica"

BEETHOVEN: Symphony No. 5
BEETHOVEN: Symphony No. 6 "Pastoral"
BEETHOVEN: Symphony No. 9 "Choral"
BORODIN: Polovetsian Dances
BRAHMS: Academic Festival Overture
BRAHMS: Hungarian Dances
BRAHMS: Piano Concerto No. 1.
BRAHMS: Piano Concerto No. 2
BRAHMS: Violin Concerto in D
BRAHMS: Concerto in A for Violin and Cello
BRAHMS: Symphony No. 1
BRAHMS: Symphony No. 2
BRAHMS: Symphony No. 3
BRAHMS: Symphony No. 4
BRITTEN: Young Person's Guide to the Orchestra
BRUCH: Scottish Fantasy
CHOPIN: Ballades
CHOPIN: Nocturnes
CHOPIN: Waltzes
COPLAND: Appalachian Spring
COPLAND: Fanfare for the Common Man
COPLAND: Rodeo
DEBUSSY: Clair de Lune
DEBUSSY: La Mer
DUKAS: Sorcerer's Apprentice
DVORAK: Cello Concerto in B Minor
DVORAK: Symphony No. 9 "New World"
DVORAK: Serenade in E Major, Op. 22
FRANCK: Symphony in D Minor
GERSHWIN: An American in Paris
GRIEG: Piano Concerto in A Minor
GRIEG: Peer Gynt Suite, Op. 46
GROFE: Grand Canyon Suite
HANDEL: Messiah
HANDEL: Water Music & Royal Fireworks Music
HAYDN: Symphony No. 94 "Surprise"
HAYDN: Symphony No. 101 "Clock"

HAYDN: Trumpet Concerto in E-flat
HOLST: The Planets
HOLST: Suite in E-flat
KHACHATURIAN: Violin Concerto
MENDELSSOHN: Violin Concerto in E Minor
MENDELSSOHN: A Midsummer Night's Dream
MENDELSSOHN: Symphony No. 4 "Italian"
MENDELSSOHN: Symphony No. 5 "Reformation"
MOZART: Piano Concerto No. 20
MOZART: Symphony No. 41 "Jupiter"
MOZART: Clarinet Quintet in A
MOZART: String Quintet in G
MOZART: Eine Kleine Nachtmusik
MUSSORGSKY: Pictures at an Exhibition
PACHELBEL: Canon in D Major
PROKOFIEV: Peter and the Wolf
RACHMANINOFF: Piano Concerto No. 2
RACHMANINOFF: Rhapsody of a Theme of Paganini
RAVEL: Bolero
RAVEL: La Valse
RAVEL: Pavane pour une infante defunte
RESPIGHI: Pines of Rome and Fountains of Rome
RIMSKY-KORSAKOV: Scheherazade
RODRIGO: Concerto de Aranjuez
SAINT-SAENS: Carnival of the Animals
SAINT-SAENS: The Organ Symphony No. 3
SCHUBERT: Symphony No. 8 "Unfinished"
SCHUBERT: String Quartet No. 14
SIBELIUS: Finlandia
SMETANA: The Moldau
SOUSA: Marches
STRAUSS, RICHARD: Waltzes
STRAUSS, JOHANN: Also Sprach Zarathustra
STRAUSS, JOHANN: Till Eulenspiegel's Merry Pranks and
        Ein Heldenleben
STRAVINSKY: Firebird Suite
TCHAIKOVSKY: 1812 Overture

TCHAIKOVSKY: Nutcracker Suite
TCHAIKOVSKY: Piano Concerto in B-Flat Minor
TCHAIKOVSKY: Romeo and Juliet
TCHAIKOVSKY: Swan Lake and Sleeping Beauty
TCHAIKOVSKY: Symphony No. 6 "Pathetique"
TCHAIKOVSKY: Serenade for Strings in C Major
VAUGHAN WILLIAMS: Fantasia on Greensleeves
VAUGHAN WILLIAMS: Rhosymedre (Lovely)
VERDI: Aida: Grand March
VIVALDI: The Four Seasons
WAGNER: Orchestral Music from the Operas
WALTON: Belshazzar's Feast

Good Recordings of Sacred Music

Especially for Children
Our Hymn Heritage, Vols 1 & 2 - Sacred Music Services

Brass
Hymns in Brass, Vols 1 & 2 - Sacred Music Services
Praise God In His Sanctuary - Paul Jones Music
Sound His Praise – Sacred Music Services
Lost in Wonder, Love, and Praise – SoundForth

Choral
Alleluia Sing! – Coventry Music
Best Loved Hymns – EMI Classics
Complete New England Hymnal, The – Priory Records
Crown Him! – Coventry Music
Faire Is the Heaven – Collegium Records
Favorite Hymns and Anthems – Gothic Records
Gloria! Music of Praise and Inspiration – Telarc
Hail, Gladdening Light – Collegium Records
Music of the English Church – Collegium Records
Hymns for a Modern Reformation – Paul Jones Music
John Rutter Collection, The – Decca

John Rutter: Gloria, and Other Sacred Music – Hyperion
John Rutter: Te Deum, and Other Church Music – Collegium Record
Joy of God, The – Marquis Music
Music for Holy Week – EMI Classics
New Music for the Church, Vol. 1 – Paul Jones Music
Oxford Church Anthems – Nimbus Records
Proclaim His Birth – SoundForth
Psalms of the Trinity Psalter, Vols 1 & 2 – IPC Press
Sing Ye Choirs Exultant: Music of Carl Schalk – Morningstar Music
Sing, Ye Heavens: Hymns for All Time – Collegium
Vaughan Williams Hymnal, A – RCA

Strings
Classical Hymns – Green Hill Productions
Hymns of Worship from Europe and America – Mulfinger
Old English Hymns - Greenhill Music
Simply Baroque – Sony
Sun of My Soul – SoundForth
With Grateful Praise – SoundForth

Orchestral
Elegant Strings - Brentwood
For God and Country - SoundForth
May Jesus Christ Be Praised – SoundForth
Our Great Savior – Sacred Music Services
Shepherds of the Delectable Mountains – Hyperion

Selected Bibliography

Adler, Mortimer J. *Six Great Ideas*. New York: Collier Books, 1981.

The American Heritage College Dictionary. Boston: Houghton Mifflin Company, 2000.

Aquinas, Thomas. *Aquinas's Shorter Summa: Saint Thomas's Own Concise Version of His Summa Theologica*. Manchester, N.H.: Sophia Institute Press, 2001.

Augustine. *The Confessions of Saint Augustine*. New Kensington, Pa.: Whitaker House, 1996.

Balthasar, Hans Urs von. *The Glory of the Lord: A Theological Aesthetics*, i, trans. Erasmo Leiva-Merikaksi. Edinburgh: Ignatius Press, 1982.

——. *Word and Revelation*. New York: Herder and Herder, 1964.

Barker, Andrew. *Greek Musical Writings*, vol. 1. Cambridge: Cambridge University Press, 1984.

Barrett, Michael P. V. *Complete In Him: A Guide to Understanding and Enjoying the Gospel*. Greenville, S.C.: Ambassador-Emerald International, 2000.

Begbie, Jeremy S. *Voicing Creation's Praise*. London: Continuum, 1991.

Bent, Ian. *Analysis*. New York: W. W. Norton & Company, 1987.

Bernstein, Leonard. *The Unanswered Question: Six Talks at Harvard*. Cambridge, Mass.: Harvard University Press, 1976.

Best, Harold M. *Music through the Eyes of Faith*. San Francisco: Harper, 1993.

Black, David Alan. "Paulus Infirmus: Pauline Concept of Weakness." *Grace Theological Journal* 5, 1 (Spring 1984).

Blackwell, Albert L. *The Sacred in Music*. Louisville: Westminster John Knox Press, 1999.

Blanchard, John and Peter Anderson. *Pop Goes the Gospel*. Darlington, England: Evangelical Press, 1989.

Bloom, Allan. *The Closing of the American Mind: How Higher Education Has Failed Democracy and Impoverished the Souls of Today's Students*. New York: Simon and Schuster, 1987.

Blume, Friedrich, et al. *Protestant Church Music: A History*. New York: W. W. Norton & Company, 1974.

Boa, Kenneth D. "What Is Behind Morality?" *Bibliotheca Sacra* 133, 530 (April 1976).

Bock, Darrell L. and Buist M. Fanning. *Interpreting the New Testament Text: Introduction to the Art and Science of Exegesis*. Wheaton: Crossway Books, 2006.

Bookman, Douglas. "The Scriptures and Biblical Counseling" in *Introduction to Biblical Counseling*, John MacArthur and Wayne A. Mack. Dallas: Word Publishing, 1994.

Bordwine, James E. *A Guide to the Westminster Confession of Faith and Larger Catechism*. Jefferson, Mass.: The Trinity Foundation, 1991.

Bouwsma, O. K. "The Expression Theory of Art," in *Aesthetics and Language*, ed. W. Elton. Oxford: Oxford University Press, 1952

Brown, Frank Burch. *Good Taste, Bad Taste, and Christian Taste: Aesthetics in Religious Life*. Oxford: University Press, 2000.

Brown, Montague. *Restoration of Reason: The Eclipse and Recovery of Truth, Goodness, and Beauty*. Grand Rapids: Baker, 2006.

Bruner, Gordon C., II. "Music, Mood, and Marketing." *Journal of Marketing* 54, 4 (October 1990): 94-104.

Buszin, Walter E. "Luther on Music." *The Musical Quarterly* 32, 1 (January 1946): 80-97.

Carroll, Joseph S. *How To Worship Jesus Christ.* Chicago: Moody, 1984.

Chafer, Lewis Sperry. "Revelation." *Bibliotheca Sacra* 94, 375 (July 1937).

Chafer, Rollin Thomas. "A Syllabus of Studies in Hermeneutics Part 6: The Relation of Logic to Interpretation." *Bibliotheca Sacra* 94, 374 (April 1937).

Childs, B. S. *Biblical Theology in Crisis.* Philadelphia: Westminster, 1976.

Contemporary Christian Music (magazine). Salem Communications Co. November 1988, 12.

Cook, Nicholas. "Schenker's Theory of Music as Ethics." *The Journal of Musicology* 7, 4 (Autumn 1989): 414-439.

Coolidge, Mary L. "Ethics—Apollonian and Dionysian." *The Journal of Philosophy* 38, 17 (Aug. 14, 1941): 449-465.

Cooper, John W. *Body, Soul & Life Everlasting: Biblical Anthropology and the Monism-Dualism Debate.* Grand Rapids: Eerdmans, 1989.

Davis, Arthur P. *Isaac Watts.* London: Independent Press, 1943.

Detwiler, David F. "Church Music and Colossians 3:16," *Bibliotheca Sacra* 158, 631 (July 2001).

Dyrness, William A. "The Imago Dei and Christian Aesthetics." *JETS* 15, 3 (Summer 1972): 161-172.

———. "Aesthetics In The Old Testament: Beauty In Context." *JETS* 28,4 (December 1985): 421-432.

Edgar, William. "Aesthetics Beauty Avenged, Apologetics Enriched." *WTJ* 63,1 (Spring 2001): 107-122.

———. *Taking Note of Music.* London: SPCK, 1986.

Edwards, Jonathan. *The "Miscellanies (Entry Nos. a–z, aa-zz, 1–500),"* ed. Thomas A. Schafer. New Haven: Yale University Press, 1994.

———. *The Nature of True Virtue.* Ann Arbor: University of Michigan Press, 1960.

———. *The Religious Affections.* Carlisle, Pa.: The Banner of Truth Trust, 2001.

———. *An Unpublished Essay of Edwards on the Trinity with Remarks on Edwards and His Theology.* ed. George P. Fisher. New York: C. Scribner's Sons, 1903.

———. "A Divine and Supernatural Light." *The Works of Jonathan Edwards.* Vol. 17, *Sermons and Discourses 1730-1733.* ed. Mark Valeri. New Haven: Yale University Press, 1999.

Elton, W., ed. *Aesthetics and Language,* Oxford: Oxford University Press, 1952.

Elliot, T. S. *Christianity and Culture.* New York: Harcourt, Brace and World, 1949.

English, William F. "An Integrationist's Critique of and Challenge to the Bobgan's View of Counseling Psychotherapy." *Journal of Psychologyy and Theology* 18, 3 (1990).

Estes, Daniel J. "Audience Analysis and Validity in Application." *Bibliotheca Sacra* 150, 598 (April 1993).

Faulkner, Quentin. *Wiser Than Despair: The Evolution of Ideas in the Relationship of Music and the Christian Church.* Westport, Conn.: Greenwood Press, 1996.

Fisher, Tim. *The Battle for Christian Music*. Greenville, S.C.: Sacred Music Services, 1992.

Forell, George W., Harold J. Grimm, and Theodore Hoelty-Nickel. *Luther and Culture*. Decorah, Iowa: Luther College, 1960.

Fowl, Stephen E. "The New Testament, Theology, and Ethics." In *Hearing the New Testament*, Green, Joel B. 394. Grand Rapids: Eerdmans, 1995.

Frame, John. *Contemporary Worship Music: A Biblical Defense*. Phillipsburg, N.J.: P & R, 1997.

———. "In Defense of Something Close to Biblicism: Reflections On *Sola Scriptura* and History in Theological Method." *Westminster Theological Journal* 59, 2 (Fall 1997).

———. "Some Questions About the Regulative Principle." *Westminster Theological Journal* 54, 2 (Fall 1992).

———. *Worship in Spirit and Truth*. Phillipsburg, N.J.: P&R, 1996.

Garlock, Frank and Kurt Woetzel. *Music in the Balance*. Greenville, S.C.: Majesty Music, 1992.

Green, Joel B. *Hearing the New Testament: Strategies for Interpretation*. Grand Rapids: Eerdmans, 1995.

Greidanus, Sidney. *The Modern Preacher and the Ancient Text: Interpreting and Preaching Biblical Literature*. Grand Rapids: Eerdmans, 1988.

Grisanti, Michael A. "The Abortion Dilemma." *Master's Theological Journal* 11, 2 (Fall 2000).

Grudem, Wayne. "Review Article: 'Should We Move beyond the New Testament to a Better Ethic?'" *Journal of the Evangelical Theological Society* 47, 2 (June 2004).

———. *Systematic Theology*. Grand Rapids: Zondervan, 1994.

Harrell, Robert Lomas. "A Comparison of Secular Elements in the Chorales of Martin Luther with Rock Elements in Church Music of the 1960's and 1970's" (M.A. Thesis, Greenville, S.C.: Bob Jones University, 1975).

Harries, Richard. *Art and the Beauty of God: A Christian Understanding*. New York: Continuum, 1993.

Herbert, George. *The Temple. Sacred Poems and Private Ejaculations*, ed. N. Ferrar. Cambridge: T. Buck and R. Daniel, 1633.

Hill, Andrew E. *Enter His Courts with Praise*. Grand Rapids: Baker, 1993.

Hodges, John Mason. "Aesthetics And The Place Of Beauty In Worship." *Reformation and Revival* 9, 3 (Summer 2000), 59-75.

———. "Beauty Revisited." *Reformation and Revival* 4, 4 (Fall 1995), 65-78.

Hodges, Zane C. "Legalism: The Real Thing." *Journal of the Grace Evangelical Society* 9, 2 (Autumn 1996).

Hospers, John, ed. *Introductory Readings in Aesthetics*. New York: The Free Press, 1969.

Hustad, Donald. *Jubilate II: Church Music in Worship and Renewal*. Carol Stream, Ill.: Hope, 1993.

Irwin, Joyce, ed. *Journal of the American Academy of Religion Thematic Studies*, vol. 50, no. 1. Chico, Calif.: Scholars Press, 1983.

Johansson, Calvin. *Discipling Music Ministry: Twenty-First Century Directions*. Peabody, Mass.: Hendrickson, 1992.

Johnson, Dennis E.. "Spiritual Antithesis: Common Grace, And Practical Theology." *Westminster Theological Journal* 64, 1 (Spring 2002).

Kaiser, Walter C. *Toward an Exegetical Theology: Biblical Exegesis for Preaching and Teaching.* Grand Rapids: Baker, 1981.

Kelly, Thomas. *Hymns on Various Passages of Scripture.* M. Moses, 1804.

Kilby, Clyde S. *Christianity and Aesthetics.* Chicago: InterVarsity Press, 1961.

Klein, William W., Craig L. Blomberg, Robert L. Hubbard, eds. *Introduction to Biblical Interpretation.* Dallas: Word Publishing, 1993.

Klug, Eugene F. "Word and Scripture in Luther Studies Since World War II." *Trinity Journal* 5, 1 (Spring 1984).

Langer, Susanne K. "The Work of Art as a Symbol" in *Introductory Readings in Aesthetics,* John Hospers. New York: The Free Press, 1969.

Lehmann, Helmut T., ed. *Luther's Works.* 55 vols. Philadelphia: Fortress, 1965.

Leupold, Ulrich S. "Learning from Luther? Some Observations on Luther's Hymns." *Journal of Church Music* 8 (July-August 1966): 5–25.

Lewis, C. S. *The Weight of Glory and Other Addresses.* Grand Rapids: Eerdmans, 1965.

———. *Reflections on the Psalms.* New York: Harcourt, Brace and World, 1958.

———. *The Four Loves.* New York: Harcourt Brace & Company, 1988.

Lindbeck, G. "Scripture, Consensus, and Community." *This World* 23 (1988).

Lindsey, F. Duane. "Essays Toward a Theology of Beauty: Part I: God Is Beautiful." *Bibliotheca Sacra* 131, 522 (April-June 1974): 120-136.

Lovelace, Austin C. *The Anatomy of Hymnody.* Chicago: G. I. A., 1965.

Luther, Martin. "Against the Heavenly Prophets in the Matter of Images and Sacraments," trans. Bernhard Erling, in *Luther's Works,* eds. Conrad Bergendoff and Helmut Lehmann, vol. 40: *Church and Ministry II,* American (Philadelphia: Muhlenberg, 1958)

———. *Works: Spiritual Hymn Book,* vol. 6.

Lutkin, Peter Christian. *Music in the Church.* New York: AMS, 1970.

MacArthur, John. *Ashamed of the Gospel.* Wheaton, Ill.: Crossway, 1993.

———. *The Ultimate Priority.* Chicago: Moody, 1983.

Mack, Wayne A. "The Sufficiency of Scripture in Counseling." *Master's Seminary Journal* 9, 1 (Spring 1998).

Maddox, T. D. F. "Scripture, Perspicuity, and Postmodernity." *Review and Expositor* 100, 4 (Fall 2003).

Makujina, John. "Forgotten Texts and Doctrines in Current Evangelical Responses to Culture." Presented at the East Region Annual Conference of The Evangelical Theological Society, March 26, 2004.

———. *Measuring the Music: Another Look at the Contemporary Music Debate.* Second edition. Willow Street, Pa.: Old Paths Publications, 2002.

Mappes, David. "The 'Elder' in the Old and New Testaments." Bsac 154, 613 (Jan-Mar 1997), 80-92.

Marshall, Molly T. "Galatians 5.1, 13-14: Free Yet Enslaved." *Review and Expositor* 91, 2 (Spring 1994).

Masters, Peter. *Worship in the Melting Pot.* London: Wakeman, 2002.

McQuilkin, J. Robertson. *Understanding and Applying the Bible.* Chicago: Moody, 1983.

——— and Bradford Mullen. "The Impact of Postmodern Thinking on Evangelical Hermeneutics." *Journal of the Evangelical Theological Society* 40, 1 (March 1997).

Meyer, Leonard B. *Emotion and Meaning in Music.* Chicago: University of Chicago Press, 1956.

Miles, Margaret. "Vision: The Eye of the Body and the Eye of the Mind in Saint Augustine's *De Trinitate* and *Confessions.*" *Journal of Religion* 63 (April, 1983): 125-42.

Miller, Steve. *The Contemporary Christian Music Debate. Worldly Compromise or Agent of Renewal?* Wheaton: Tyndale House, 1993.

Montgomery, John Warwick. "Lessons from Luther On The Inerrancy Of Holy Writ's." *Westminster Theological Journal* 36, 3 (Spring 1974).

———. "The Approach of New Shape Roman Catholicism To Scriptural Inerrancy: A Case Study for Evangelicals." *Journal of the Evangelical Theological Society* 10, 4 (Fall 1967).

Muller, Richard A. "Historiography in the Service of Theology and Worship: Toward Dialogue with John Frame." *Westminster Theological Journal* 59, 2 (Fall 1997).

Murray, John. "The Weak and the Strong." *Westminster Theological Journal* 12, 2 (May 1950).

Myers, Kenneth A. *All God's Children and Blue Suede Shoes: Christians & Popular Culture.* Wheaton: Crossway, 1989.

Nettle, Paul. *Luther and Music.* New York: Russell & Russell, 1967.

Noebel, David A. *Christian Rock: A Stategem of Mephistopheles.* Manitou Springs, Colo.: Summit Ministries, n.d.

Noll, Mark A. *America's God: From Jonathan Edwards to Abraham Lincoln.* Oxford: Oxford University Press, 2002.

Osborne, Grant R. *The Hermeneutical Spiral: A Comprehensive Introduction to Biblical Interpretation.* Revised, expanded ed. Downers Grove, Ill.: InterVarsity Press, 2006.

Pareles, Jon. "Metallica Defies Heavy Metal Stereotypes," *Minneapolis Star Tribune*, 13 July 1988.

Pascal, Blaise, trans. by W. F. Trotter. *Pascal's Pensées.* New York: E. P. Dutton, 1958.

Payton, Leonard, R. "Congregational Singing And The Ministry Of The Word." *Revival and Reformation* 7, 1 (Winter 1998): 119-166.

Pearcey, Nancy. *Total Truth: Liberating Christianity from its Cultural Captivity.* Wheaton: Crossway, 2005.

Pettegrew, Larry. "Theological Basis of Ethics." *Master's Theological Journal* 11, 2 (Fall, 2000).

Piper, John. *Desiring God: Meditations of a Christian Hedonist.* Sisters, Ore.: Multnomah Books, 1996.

———. *God's Passion for His Glory: Living the Vision of Jonathan Edwards: With the Complete Text of "The End For Which God Created The World" by Jonathan Edwards*. Wheaton: Crossway Books, 1998.

Plass, Edwald M., ed. *What Luther Says*. St. Louis: Concordia, 1959.

Pontynen, Arthur. *For the Love of Beauty: Art, History, and the Moral Foundations of Aesthetic Judgment*. London: Transaction Publishers, 2006.

Ralston, Timothy J. "Showing the Relevance: Application, Ethics, and Preaching" in *Interpreting the New Testament Text: Introduction to the Art and Science of Exegesis*, Bock, Darrell L. and Buist M. Fanning. 293. Wheaton: Crossway Books, 2006.

Reimer, Bennett. *A Philosophy of Music Education: Advancing the Vision*. 3. Upper Saddle River, N.J.: Prentice-Hall, 2003.

Reynolds, William J. *A Survey of Christian Hymnody*. Carol Stream: Hope, 1999.

Richard, Ramesh P. "Methodological Proposals for Scripture Relevance: Part 2: Levels of Biblical Meaning." *Bibliotheca Sacra* 143, 570 (April 1986).

Riches, John, ed.. *The Analogy of Beauty. The Theology of Hans Urs Von Balthasar*. Edinburgh: T&T Clark, 1986.

Riedel, Johannes. *The Lutheran Chorale: Its Basic Traditions*. Minneapolis: Augsburg Fortress Publishers, 1967.

Robinson, Haddon. "The Heresy of Application." *Leadership Journal* 18 (Fall, 1997).

Routley, Eric. *The Music of Christian Hymns*. Chicago: G.I.A. Publications, 1981.

Ryrie, Charles C. *Basic Theology*. Wheaton: Victor, 1988.

Schaff, Phillip. *The Creeds of Christendom*. Grand Rapids: Baker, 2007.

Schalk, Carl, ed. *Key Words in Church Music*. St. Louis: Concordia, 1978.

Scruton, Roger. *Culture Counts: Faith and Feeling in a World Besieged*. New York: Encounter Books, 2007.

Shaftesbury, Anthony Lord. *Characteristics of Men, Manners, Opinions, Times*. Vol. 2. Oxford: Clarendon Press, 1999.

Sharp, Cecil. *English Folk-Song: Some Conclusions*. London: Simpkin, 1907.

Sherry, Patrick. *Spirit and Beauty*. London: SCM Press, 2002.

Sloboda, John. *The Musical Mind: The Cognitive Psychology of Music*. Oxford: Clarendon, 1985.

Songer, Harold S. "Problems Arising from the Worship of Idols: 1 Corinthians 8.1-11.1." *Review and Expositor* 80, 3 (Summer 1983).

Spiegel, James S. "Aesthetics and Worship." *Southern Baptist Journal of Theology* (Winter, 1998): 40–57.

Sproul, R. C. *The Consequences of Ideas: Understanding the Concepts that Shaped Our World*. Wheaton: Crossway, 2000.

———. "The Recovery of Worship." *Reformation and Revival* 2, 1 (Winter 1993): 23-42.

Spurgeon, C. H. "Psalm the Hundred and Forty-Ninth" in *The Treasury of David*, Vol. IV: *Psalms 90-103*. Grand Rapids: Baker Book House.

Selected Bibliography

Stallard, Mike. "Literal Interpretation: The Key to Understanding the Bible." *Journal of Ministry and Theology* 4, 1 (Spring, 2000).

Stephens, W. P. *Zwingli: An Introduction to His Thought.* New York: Oxford University Press, 1992.

Swindoll, Charles R. *The Grace Awakening.* Dallas: Word, 1990.

Tagg, Philip. *Fernando the Flute.* Goteborg, Sweden: Gothenberg University, 1981.

Tarnas, Richard. *The Passion of the Western Mind: Understanding the Ideas That Have Shaped Our World View.* New York: Ballantine Books, 1991.

Thomas, Robert L. "General Revelation and Biblical Hermeneutics." *Master's Seminary Journal* 9, 1 (Spring 1998).

Tiessen, Terrance. "Toward a Hermeneutic for Discerning Universal Moral Absolutes." *Journal of the Evangelical Theological Society* 36, 2 (June 1993).

Tozer, A. W. *Whatever Happened to Worship?* Camp Hill, Pa.: Christian Publications, Inc., 1985.

Van Til, Cornelius. *The Defense of the Faithfulness.* Philadelphia: Presbyterian and Reformed, 1963.

Vanhoozer, Kevin J. "A Lamp In The Labyrinth: The Hermeneutics Of 'Aesthetic' Theology." *Trinity Journal* 8, 1 (Spring 1987): 25-56.

Viladesau, Richard. *Theological Aesthetics: God in Imagination, Beauty, and Art.* New York: Oxford, 1999.

Warren, Timothy S. "A Paradign for Preaching." *Bibliotheca Sacra* 148, 592 (October 1991).

———. "The Theological Process in Sermon Preparation." *Bibliotheca Sacra* 156, 623 (July 1999).

Watts, Isaac. *The Psalms of David Imitated in the Language of the New Testament, and Applied to the Christian State and Worship.* (http://www.ccel.org/cceh/archives/eee/wattspre.htm).

Weil, Simone, trans. by Elisabeth Chase Geissbuhler. *Intimations of Christianity among the Ancient Greeks.* London: Routledge and Kegan Paul, 1957.

Weiss, Piero and Richard Taruskin, *Music in the Western World: A History in Documents.* Belmont, Calif.: Schirmer, 1984.

Whiteley, Sheila, ed. *Sexing the Groove: Popular Music and Gender,* New York: Routledge, 1997.

Wiersbe, Warren W. *Real Worship.* Grand Rapids: Baker, 2000.

Young, Carlton R. et al. *Duty and Delight: Routley Remembered.* Carol Stream, Ill.: Hope Publishing, 1985.

Yount, Terry. "Musical Taste: The Ultimate Sacrifice?" *Reformation and Revival* 4, 4 (Fall 1995): 79-90.

Zuck, Roy B. "The Role of the Holy Spirit in Hermeneutics." *Bibliotheca Sacra* 141, 562 (April 1984).

Scripture Index

271

1 Corinthians (cont.)
3:16-17 154
6:11. 37
6:12. 41
6:18. 136
8:1. 21
8-10. . . . . 4, 39
8:9. 41
9:27. . . . . 42, 54
10:23-24 40
10:31. . . . 21, 40, 121,
          149, 239
10:32-33 41
11:8-9 11
14:23 152
14:25. 184
14:29. 118
16:8. 61

2 Corinthians
1:3. 177
6:4-10 209

Galatians
5:19-21 . . . . 10, 136
6:4. 118

Ephesians
1 243
1:1-11 192
1:7. 177
1:11 239
2:4. 177
2:10 37
2:14-16 192
2:19-22 153
4:11-16 160
4:29 136
5:3-7 136-137
5:10. 118
5:19 . . . . . . 165, 167

Philippians
1:6. 37
1:9-11 38
1:10. 117
2:6-11 191
2:12-13 38
3:3. . . . . 28, 29
4:4 209
4:4-7 209
4:8 . . . . . . 118, 137

Colossians
1:15-20 192
3:8. 137
3:10-14 38
3:16. 167
3:23 iii

1 Thessalonians
1:9. 177
5:6. 213
5:21. 117

2 Thessalonians
1:9-10 241

1 Timothy
3:2. 213
3:16. 191-192

2 Timothy
2:11-13 192
3:16-17 . . 3, 8, 16, 21

Titus
2:6. 213
2:12. 38

Hebrews
1:3. 192
5:11-14 10
5:14. 118
10:25 152

James
1:17. 177
2:14. 56
3:17-18 38
5:13. 165

1 Peter
1 56
1:3-4, 7 38
1:8. 211
1:13. 213
1:15-16 177
2:5, 9 154
2:13-14 6
2:17. 6
4:11 240
5:8. 213
5:10. 177

2 Peter
1:3-11 39
1:21. 2

1 John
2:12 243
3:2. 38
3:6-9 48
3:20 177
4:8. 177
5:18. 49

Revelation
4-5. 237
4:10. 28
4:11. . . . . . . 238, 239
5:9ff 165
19:6. 177

Subject / Name Index